Through the Darkness

Glimmers of Healing Hope

Through the Darkness

Darkness

Glimmers of Healing Hope

Adolfo Quezada

✛ ABBEY PRESS

Cover Design:
Scott Wannemuehler

Library of Congress Catalog Number
92-74491

ISBN 0-87029-256-0

©1993 by Adolfo Quezada
Published by Abbey Press
St. Meinrad Archabbey
St. Meinrad, Indiana 47577

Printed in the United States of America

*T*o you who at this very hour are lost in the darkness of a troubled life, who suffer from a broken heart, a confused mind, or a wounded soul.

Contents

Preface

*T*he clouds are dark this day and the world is ugly. Life is not a place to be. The pain of it all is more than we can bear, and we are tempted to despair.

Then it appears, the small and beautiful hummingbird, moving to and fro, singing its morning song. We feel lost and hopeless, but this little godly creature gives us a piece of hope that will sustain us through the day.

But why? The hummingbird has not solved our problems; it has not taken the pain away. What is so different from before?

Somehow the sight of so much energy exuding from such a small source sparks a belief that this energy is also in us, however small. We come to believe—for just that moment—that, no matter how bad things are and regardless of our circumstances, there is within us an ember that will not burn out, a life that will not give up, and a possibility that will not be stifled.

Through the Darkness is about such faith. It is a book that confronts the pain and suffering of life in the light of our spirituality. From the fear of "abandonment" to the reality of "victimization," we are a broken people. This book offers a new perspective through which we can gain back what we have lost. It is grounded in the belief that we have within us a force that heals, if we but allow it to do its work. When we seek the power from within, we are lifted out of ourselves and carried toward wholeness.

The little glimmers of light, the small cracks of dawn, and the tiny shreds of hope are all that we need to make it through the darkest of nights. In the midst of our doubt, we can believe. From the pit of despair, we can hope. Wherever there can be found even one tiny cell that is alive, there is the possibility of abundant life.

Come, little hummingbird; sing your song. Let the world know that God is little and that if we would hear God, we must listen for a still, small voice; that if we would see God, we must look for little signs; and that if we would come to God, we must be little too.

Abandonment

*T*he terror invades every fiber of our being; the fear of abandonment returns.

Even as adults we respond to life according to our early childhood experiences, and for many of us, being left behind by someone we love and need is a fate worse than death. Nothing seems as devastating to us as abandonment, and nothing has the same long-lasting effect. Whether real or imagined, our experiences of separation in early life have a

5

strong effect on the way we live today.

Separation from our mothers as infants is our first confrontation with major loss. Such separation happens slowly and naturally. Abandonment is experienced when the separation is sudden and long-lasting. Whether mother leaves for an extended time or permanently, whether she leaves physically or emotionally, we are deprived of the security, nurturance, and basic human connection that sustain us.

If we are deprived, for whatever reason, of this early connection, we may have an emotional reaction that contributes to dysfunctional behavior in later life.

If we did not establish this vital mother-child bond, we may have grown up believing that we are unlovable. If all our life we have felt unloved, then we probably do not know how to love. This has a great influence on our relationships. Unresolved issues of abandonment keep us in fear of being hurt again. We

may have difficulty establishing one-to-one relationships and may suffer from poor self-
esteem and low self-confidence. We may find
it difficult to build trust or to ask others for
help. And every time we experience a loss
through death, it taps all of our childhood
fears of abandonment, which disrupts our nor-
mal grieving process.

Just as a child detaches emotionally from
an absent parent even after the parent returns,
we, as adults, protect ourselves this way. We
assume a posture of self-reliance and independence that is supposed to save us from
further abandonment, but which only assures
us of continued isolation and loneliness.

Another way we protect ourselves from
the pain of abandonment is to spend our lives
taking care of others. We decide that, instead
of hurting as we do, we will numb our pain by
throwing ourselves into compulsive care-
taking.

Those of us who fear abandonment sometimes hide behind our smiles. We act as if the world is our oyster and nothing and no one can harm us. We tend to be loners and trust no one. We run away from any form of intimacy because we do not want to be hurt again. We feel guilty about good things that happen to us because we do not believe we deserve them. Besides, we reason, there is always the probability that what we have we will lose anyway. We fear anything we believe will lead to abandonment. Some women fear success because they believe men will abandon them. Some men fear failure because they believe women will abandon them.

As adults we are unconsciously aware of the tremendous pain of abandonment that we felt early on. With this pain comes despair and rage. If we leave it untreated, or worse, if we turn it in on ourselves, it results in a state of depression.

Depression sets in whenever something reminds us of the loneliness, sadness, help-

8

lessness, and hopelessness that we felt as a child. We opt for the emptiness of depression over the agony of abandonment. Depression dulls us to the pain of loss.

The problem with protecting ourselves against the pain of abandonment through detachment, depression, or rage is that we end up abandoning ourselves. There is no loneliness greater than separation from ourselves.

The road to emotional health must be paved with self-love that gives to us what we did not get before. Through self-love we begin to protect the scared child within. We love and nurture that hurting child. We embrace and accept that lost child. We promise to stay with that abandoned child.

We can do this only if we are willing to turn to God for the power to love ourselves unconditionally. It is from our connectedness to God that we derive our connectedness to ourselves. Once we believe in God's unconditional love for us and in our un-

9

conditional love for ourselves, we are then able to establish the necessary connectedness with others.

As we live, we will continue to experience loss and separation, and it will hurt. But standing on the firm ground of God's commitment to us, we will deal with what comes our way with the faith that we are not alone.

Accepting Ourselves

God grant us the courage to be ourselves and to live and act according to our natural being, regardless of what others may think about us.

Many of us live life in constant fear of looking foolish in the eyes of others. We do everything in our power to hide from others those parts of ourselves that may prove embarrassing or self-disclosing.

We work overtime to manage the image we reveal to the world, making sure that others see only what we want them to see and think only what we want them to think.

This self-consciousness, this full-time pre-occupation with ourselves, stifles our natural personalities and kills the spontaneity that is essential for holistic living. When we take ourselves too seriously, we lose flexibility and genuineness. We block our natural responses to life's events and end up manipulating and controlling our environment, including ourselves and others.

This inordinate need for image management and control comes from the fear of being humiliated, that is, reduced to a lower position in our own eyes or the eyes of others. Sometimes this fear stems from humiliating experiences we had in childhood.

After such experiences, we may have vowed never to allow ourselves to be humiliated again. Our way to avoid this has been to exert tight control over ourselves in every situation.

In adulthood, our fear of humiliation has grown into fear of imperfection, and our fear of looking foolish has grown into fear of looking bad. Our main concern has become: "What will people say?" Our belief has become: "If they see the imperfect part of me, they will disapprove."

Our fear of humiliation is real. Humiliation does leave emotional scars. We can't just talk ourselves out of this fear. The antidote is new experience that replaces our old, devastating experience.

Through prayer we come to love God, ourselves, and others. Through love we receive the courage to be our true selves, regardless of the real or imagined impressions we may make on others. We dare to act childlike, look foolish, and be different. We risk the ridicule of others and their disapproval. We do this not without fear, but through our fear.

As we let go of our control over the image we portray to others, we bring back the spontaneity and authenticity that make life worth living. We even have more fun.

Humility does not mean that we allow others to humiliate us. It means that we have the courage to be our total selves and embrace our strengths and weaknesses, our assets and liabilities, our impressive and unimpressive qualities, and our serious and silly sides.

What we discover is that when we accept ourselves as we are and act accordingly, others are likely to accept us as well. But even if they don't, we remain centered in the self-acceptance that is part of our self-love.

Addiction

*S*ome of us are shackled with the chains of addiction; all of us are bound by the ropes of attachment.

Whether we know it or not, we are worshipping false gods every day of our lives. We may live religiously oriented lives, and we may pay lip service to loving God with all our heart, mind, and soul. But in the real moments of daily life, we dedicate ourselves to the gods who really matter to us. Whatever extracts from us our attention, time, energy, resources,

15

and allegiance is the god we choose to worship. We need to acknowledge this.

We need to recognize the object of our obsession and compulsion, the subject of our preoccupation, and the focus of our will and desire. Only when we see clearly that which attracts us strongly will we be able to deal with it effectively.

We need to become aware of reality and not allow ourselves to stay in denial. Blinded by our pride, we fail to see how low we have fallen, and fixated on control, we don't realize how out of control we have become. The more control we attempt to exercise, the more addicted we become; the more addicted we become, the more control we try to exercise. We must come to realize that this vicious cycle of control and addiction cannot be broken by willpower or stronger efforts on our part.

Let us move toward the freedom that is our inheritance and get on the path that takes us through dark valleys, treacherous mountains, arid deserts, and frightful forests. Let us walk the path of self-surrender.

In our surrender, let us not deliver ourselves to the power of our false gods; yet, neither let us rely on our own power to overcome. We must understand that we are without power in the struggle for our lives.

The power of God is the only power on which we can truly rely: the power that can pluck us out of the pit of despair in which we find ourselves and set us in the place of fruitful living.

In our surrender, we face up to the harm we have caused by living outside the realm of love, and we seek forgiveness from our victims as well as from ourselves.

Focused only on God, our lives will change because we will change. Our chains and ropes will fall away, and in their place we will don the cloak of freedom fit for the children of Unconditional Love.

In our surrender, we guard against a return to self-sufficiency. We remain forever vigilant of our precarious perch on the cliff of life. We remember that only through a constant awareness of our vulnerability to the lure of false gods will we cling for dear life to God's guiding hand. Let prayer be our daily bread and meditation be our milk.

We receive the gift of love and it transforms our life; but it is more than we can keep, and we must share it with another. As we give it away, it comes back to us in manifold ways, and thus the circle of love is closed.

Becoming

Let us focus not so
much on what we have been or even on what
we may be. Instead, let us dare to embrace the
glorious state of our becoming.

In an attempt to understand ourselves we
look at the past, and in hope of bettering ourselves we look at the future. Thus we divide
ourselves in two and lose the unity of our eternal self.

The concept of *the present* is nothing more
than a concept, for in reality the moment will

not be captured. It flows on with the river of time.

Such is the state of the human personality. It will not be frozen. We are in a dynamic state of transition. Each of us is in perpetual growth, and although we may describe who we are in general terms, it is impossible to confine ourselves to time, space, or condition. Even as we attempt to do so, we have already moved on.

We are not our past nor our future. We are the becoming that joins both in the unity of forever. It is with this spirit of our endless becoming that we must identify to stay alive. If we limit ourselves to what we have been, we condemn ourselves to the prison of yesterday. If we imagine ourselves as what we may be, our lives are but fantasy. Only in the state of becoming will we find our true identity. Only in the process of growth will we discover our reality.

We are the unfolding roses of morning. We

are the changing hues of sunset. We are the growing children of God. In the state of becoming there is transgression and forgiveness. In the miracle of transformation there are endings and beginnings. In the midst of ethereal life there is the constancy of God.

As we embrace the state of becoming, we dare to celebrate the temporary, which is all we really have. In the temporary we smell the rose, we watch the hummingbird, we listen to the wind. In the temporary we hold dear the little child, for tomorrow the child will be gone.

In the temporary we appreciate the gift of others as their lives intersect with ours and move on. We love them and they love us back; then we free them from our grasp.

As we embrace the state of becoming, we dare to let go of being. We come to realize that we are not a thing, but an event in the life of God. We let go of everything to which only a static thing can be attached, and surrender to the vicissitudes of life.

We have held fast to the illusion of constancy because we have feared death. As we embrace the state of becoming, we release our hold on the status quo and place our faith in the constancy of God alone.

Boundaries

What are the boundaries of the soul? Where do we stop and others begin? How do we know our own identities? These are not easy questions to answer because we are products of a society that discourages the formation of a strong and definable self.

Even as children, we have been taught to deny personal feelings by suppressing them. And since the only way we come to know ourselves, or others come to know us, is through the expression of the way we feel, we often do not know who we are.

This has led to the disintegration of our boundaries, and a confusion between ourselves and others. Some of us call this love or intimacy, but in reality it is nothing more than an enmeshment of personalities. True love or intimacy can exist only between persons who are well grounded in their own identities.

Many marriages, unfortunately, are based on the loss of boundaries between partners. Instead of allowing each personality to develop on its own, two personalities are thrown together in the name of "togetherness," and either one is overpowered by the other or they are both lost in a vague and unworkable conglomeration. This loss of boundaries is not limited to marriages. It also happens between parents and their children, between other family members, and between friends.

Because of the way we have been conditioned, we have developed a fear of autonomy and independence. This separation anxiety is based on the real or imagined risk we take, whenever we assert our individuality, of being rejected or otherwise separated from the one with whom we have become enmeshed.

Togetherness is something we need to strive for as human beings. Bonding with others calls us to go out of ourselves in love and share a piece of who we are with our beloved. This is one of the greatest joys a human being can experience. But unless we first come to know and respect our own boundaries, we are giving away something we never possessed.

To know our boundaries means that we know for what we are responsible and for what we are not. It means we are aware that we have control over ourselves and no one else. It means that we feel comfortable with our individuality and appreciate the "otherness" of our beloved. It means that we are not threatened by the developing self-sufficiency of another, that, in fact, we encourage it.

To know our boundaries means that we are secure when we are separated from those we love because, although we enjoy their presence, our sense of self is not contingent on it. It means that we can be lovingly detached from those we love and thereby allow intimacy as well as separateness, oneness as well as aloneness.

Brokenness

In the breaking of the heart, we come to know the spirit within. It is a paradox of life that when we are most broken, we have the greatest opportunity for wholeness; when we are most lost in darkness, we can see even the faintest glimmer of light; and when we are deepest in the pit of despair, we discover there the roots of our faith.

Who of us has not at some point felt anguish from the blows of life? Who of us has not felt abandoned by friends and surrounded by enemies? These are the times when everything seems to be closing in on us, when we feel empty spiritually and full of debilitating stress.

How much more of this can we take? Even as we fall to the ground, the vultures want our flesh. We pray for relief, but no relief comes; we beg for deliverance, but we are not delivered.

We want to be healed, we want to mend the broken pieces of our souls, we want the cup of suffering to pass from us, yet it is not to be. Instead, we are to ask for one thing only— the surrender of our beings to God. With this surrender, which comes of grace, comes the wholeness that is unattainable through human effort. With this surrender comes the light that guides us on the paths of the spirit; and with this surrender comes a faith in, not a God of rescue and restoration, but a God who would love and live in us, even through our trials and tribulations.

As we surrender, we come to discover that the God who loves us has been with us all along. But as long as we were self-sufficient, as long as we were preoccupied with the issues of life, and as long as we believed ourselves to be whole and intact, we did not recognize God.

It is only in our brokenness that we have nothing left to lose and are willing to be humble and real. It is in our brokenness that we are willing to be transformed, that we are focused on new priorities, and that we lose our trust in the external and turn inward for our needs. From the vulnerability of our brokenness, we are finally able to understand that God enters the world through broken hearts.

Burnout

*B*urnout is the imbalance of the yin and yang of life. It is a state in which we feel overwhelmed by the stress that confronts us and lose our enthusiasm for living and doing.

In Chinese cosmology, *yin* is the feminine principle in nature that is exhibited in darkness, cold, and wetness. *Yang* is the masculine active principle exhibited in light, heat, and dryness. Yin and yang combine to produce all that comes to be.

When, because of external demands placed on us or unrealistic self-imposed expectations, we overextend ourselves for a long period of time, we burn out. We exhaust our energies. It doesn't happen all at once but slowly, over time, as we experience unceasing stress and pressure.

Our yang energy moves us to work, to produce, and to venture into the world assertively. It is the fire within that motivates us to do. Our yin energy is the more receptive part of us. It is the more courageous in that it is willing to be vulnerable and dependent. Without the yang energy, we become sentimental and needy; without the yin energy, we become machine-like, one-dimensional, and dry. If yang is the flame, yin is the oil with which it burns.

Burnout happens when we allow the oil to run so low that the flame begins to flicker or is extinguished altogether. We have allowed our emotional response to be used up without providing for a source of replenishment.

We are often unaware of, or in denial about, our collision course with burnout. Many of us respond to burnout by trying harder, working longer, and attempting to overcome what we perceive as weakness. Fortunately, our need for more yin energy will not be ignored or denied. Eventually it lets itself be known, even if it has to do so in painful ways.

In burnout, we experience a mild form of depression that results from turning in on ourselves the anger we have at not being able to accomplish all that we "should." We also experience a feeling of disillusionment or a sense of failure as a person. Sometimes in burnout we feel helpless and full of self-doubt. Or we may feel guilty for not doing things as perfectly as we expect. We become apathetic, have difficulty concentrating, and are disoriented and confused.

Burnout is manifested physically in a my-

riad of somatic disorders, including back-
aches, neck pains, headaches, insomnia, loss of
or excessive appetite, ulcers, high blood pressure, constant colds, digestive problems, al-
lergies, heart attacks, and strokes. During
burnout, many of us turn to alcohol and other
drugs—prescription and otherwise—for relief.
But drugs will only mask the burnout symp-
toms and will worsen the problem in the long
run.

In burnout, we have lost the balance between our yin and yang energies and, in the
process, have lost our spiritual perspective
and sense of limitations. Operating strictly
from our yang energy, we become prideful
and self-sufficient. We lose humility, the ability to see ourselves in the light of reality, with
all our capabilities and limitations.

The antidote for burnout is to get in touch
with our yin energy. This is the fountain of
our love for others and also the source of our
self-love. Staying with our yin energy means

that we love ourselves enough to receive what we need.

First and foremost, we need to connect with God. We need to communicate with and rest in God. We need to take the time to pray regularly and profoundly. We need to be open to all the gifts that God bestows upon us, including the beauty of nature, the nurturing love of family and friends, and the creativity that God inspires within us.

Our yin energy prompts us to take care of ourselves by eating right, exercising, playing, learning, resting, and asking—ourselves and others—for what we need. Our yin energy helps us to focus on our unique purpose in life, that which gives meaning to our days. This means that the goals and objectives that we set for ourselves must be realistic and attainable.

When we listen to our bodies and minds, we learn about the priorities of the soul. Our yin energy tells us that we need to survive before we can be of service to others and that we need love and nurturing, a sense of belonging, recognition, encouragement, support, and acceptance from others.

Our yin energy allows us to recognize our humanness and our brokenness. If we are wounded, we need to remember our condition and do whatever is necessary to heal.

Once our lamps have been filled with the oil of yin, the yang flame will burn with enthusiasm for life. We will come to understand that to *do*, we first must *be*.

Caretaking

All of us need to be needed, but God save the world from the menace of our inordinate need to be for others. In the name of good parenting, Christian service, or good old neighborliness, we sometimes overdo for others to the point of doing damage to them and to ourselves.

The overwhelming desire to be involved in the lives of our loved ones, and even of those beyond our immediate circle, may come from a cup of love that overflows. More likely, however, it is an unconscious effort on our part to fill a hole in our own lives. The hole is the lack of significance that we have attributed to ourselves as persons throughout our lives.

We may have concluded that the only way to justify our existence is to be doing for others and to help them in every way we can. Unfortunately, this also means that we need to control their lives in order to make them better.

No one can really control another person's life, and the attempt to do so results in resentment, conflict, and alienation—the very opposite of the appreciation we seek in the first place.

How do we overdo for others? We offer or agree to do for them what they are perfectly capable of doing for themselves. The payoff to us, although we may not want to admit it, is their growing dependence on us and, with it, our growing control over them.

We may play the role of martyr as we sacrifice our time, our energy, and sometimes our health in order to be available to those who "need" us. The virtue that we attach to sacrifice legitimizes this way of life for us, but in reality we may be using our sacrifice to induce guilt and thereby hook the other into our control.

Another way of doing for others to the point of detriment is to allow them to take advantage of us and treat us without respect and consideration. Forgiving mistakes comes from love, but allowing perpetual mistreatment by others comes from fear of confrontation, fear of being rejected or unloved.

In both the Hebrew and Christian Scriptures we are asked to "love your neighbor as yourself." Thus, to truly love and be for others selflessly, we must first love and be for ourselves.

Loving ourselves means accepting who we are without having to justify our existence by what we do for others. Loving ourselves means discovering our identity without having to look to others to tell us who we are. Loving ourselves means embracing our individuality and acknowledging our existential aloneness. While we may grow in communal life, we do not depend on attachment to another for our fulfillment.

To love our neighbor as ourselves means that we stop using others to avoid facing and dealing with our unfinished business. Our fulfillment must come not from how others see us, but from how we see ourselves, alone, yet full of God.

Childlikeness

*A*s children, we dare
to be ourselves—nothing more, nothing less.
A little child's outlook on the world is humble.
A child accepts himself as he is; a child does
not pretend or aspire to be other than who she
is.

Gentleness, simplicity, and humility are
characteristics of a little child. But we are
afraid to approach life as a child because we
don't want to be seen as weak, foolish, or helpless. A child is direct, trusting, affectionate,

and accepting. But we are afraid to be as a child lest we be vulnerable, emotional, or compromised.

We are as little children when we set aside our pretentious self-sufficiency and allow ourselves to receive the offerings of others, when we settle into our own simplicity and forget our attempt to live according to public opinion, and when we drop our defensiveness and confess to ourselves and to each other our vulnerability and fear of being hurt.

The child in us sees life with a special clarity that is unpolluted by suspicions, ambitions, insecurities, and prejudices. Life is yet a wonder to a child; hence, her reverence for everything about it.

As children, we forgive more easily. We are excited about life and embrace with enthusiasm all that it offers us. As children, we are willing to be led, to be spontaneous, to experience life fully.

The child in us knows nothing about God,

yet lives in purity as God's son or daughter. He does not study nature, yet is fascinated by a tree, absorbed with the intricacies of a flower, and awed by the antics of a hummingbird.

The child does not love humanity, yet she adores her daddy and mommy and embraces those who show her love. There is no planning for a child, only the surprises of spontaneity. There is no bind of ethical obligations, only the freedom of reality. A life that allows the child within to live dares us to stay in the present moment and live it completely.

It is not innocence or naiveté to which we are called. We are not asked to leave reason and maturity at the door. Rather, we are to embrace our joyous, free-spirited, creative child as part of our wholeness.

As children, we are dependent on one source. We ask for everything from God. In God's arms we have no cares, we are without distress, and we expect and receive only love.

Child Within

Who will love the little child? It is so easy to respond to the needs of the little one. Who can refuse the sweet, innocent face of a child? Who is not quick to help in any situation that involves the welfare of children? Children are special and need our protection.

We would go to the ends of the world to protect our own children and grandchildren. We live for them and would die for them. Yet, who will love the little child who abides within each one of us? Who will even acknowledge his presence or respond to her needs?

There is a child within. It is the little boy or girl from long ago who even now reaches out for the love he or she did not get before. It is this child within who reminds us daily of needs unmet, of gaps unfilled through life. It is this child who will not be consoled until he has tasted the fruit of unconditional love.

It is also this child who will block the path toward adult maturity and sabotage the efforts of others to be for us and love us.

From the moment we are born, we have basic human needs that must be met. When they are not met, they become gaping holes in our personalities that affect us and those around us. We need to be held. We need to be stroked. We need to be fussed over and treated as though we were significant. We need to be talked to, to be told that we are loved and cherished. We need to be nourished and cared for. We need to feel safe and secure. We need to be smiled upon and laughed with, and we need to experience fun and frolic. We need to be encouraged, validated, and affirmed. We need to belong, to have a sense that we are a part of the whole.

Sometimes these needs go unmet because those who are supposed to meet them don't know how to, or they simply forget. But the little child within us doesn't forget, and continues her relentless search for that unconditional love.

It would have been nice if our needs had been fulfilled many years ago, but they were not. Our first step is to recognize that fact and accept it. Then we must let go of the expectations that these needs will be met by those who were supposed to meet them, and we must forgive those people for their failure to do so.

Who will love the little child? We must. It is up to us to accept that child as one who is hurt and resentful because he was so deprived. It is up to us to realize that we cannot heal until we work through that pain and resentment. It is we who must hold that little child gently in our arms and nurture her with unconditional love. It is difficult for us to love ourselves because we've been conditioned not to. Yet, we are comforted by the belief that it is really God who loves that little child through us.

As we love the little child within, the child becomes lovable, a quality the child didn't believe he possessed. As the child begins to feel lovable, she dares to receive love from us and from others. As the child receives love, he becomes fulfilled and free from the chains that have kept him from growing up.

As we work through the unfinished business of our past, we come to understand the intensity behind some of our adult emotions and behaviors. We do not forget the painful memories of our youth, but through forgiveness we are capable of overcoming the power that unmet needs have had in our lives.

We do not stop needing the unconditional love that is essential to all human beings, but we are capable of getting that love from ourselves and from the God within. As we love God, we come to love ourselves. As we love ourselves, we come to love God.

Courage

The skies grow dark and bad times menace, and we are tempted to despair. Yet through the clouds and adversity comes the power of divine encouragement.

It is our human nature to cry out of the depths of tribulation to a source beyond ourselves. And it has been the human experience to receive the needed comfort in response. The courage that comes does not chase away fear and despair; it simply gives us the determination and perseverance to negotiate the dangerous curves and navigate the tumultuous waves.

Courage gives us the capacity to move ahead despite fear and despair. It fills us with the energy to live the day in the midst of trouble without falling into stagnation, paralysis, and depression. Courage is not given only to the lion-hearted warriors on the battlefield. It is not held exclusively by those who perform great feats of valor. Courage is a gift offered by God to all who will receive it. It is the key ingredient for coping with life.

Courage is defined by Webster as "mental or moral strength to resist opposition…firmness of mind and will in the face of danger or extreme difficulty…a quality of temperament that enables one to hold one's own against opposition, interference, or temptation."

Courage is found in the woman who faces cancer on a moment-by-moment basis— enduring pain, persevering through anxiety,

dealing with cancer's devastating consequences, and living her life to the fullest.
From her we learn that to have courage is to
be grounded in something beyond ourselves.
In spite of her brokenness, her faith makes her
whole.

Courage is found in the woman who enters reluctantly into the world of the divorced.
She risks loneliness, insecurity, and the anxiety of the unknown in order to leave what she
knows to be a safe, secure, and populated prison. From her we learn that courage is based on
our beliefs. If we believe in ourselves and our
ability to function, we will live and act courageously.

Courage is found in the mother who has
had more than her share of misfortune, yet
lives as though she were the luckiest woman
in the world. From her we learn that a courageous person looks at any situation in terms
of possible solutions and actions, rather than
dangers and threats. Courage enables us to

turn problems into challenges and crises into opportunities.

Courage is found in the man who faces prison and public disgrace for speaking and acting against injustice. From him we learn that through courage we hold to certain values and remain true to them in the face of adversity. Courage empowers us to speak up for what we believe is right and to live according to our beliefs.

Courage is found in the man who acknowledges his dependency on alcohol, seeks and receives treatment, and lives a fulfilling life as a recovering alcoholic. From him we learn that courage helps us die to our false gods so that we may embrace what really counts. Courage enables us to let go of that which impedes growth and maturity so that we may reach our full potential as human beings.

Courage is found in the man who has begun to drop his mask and become known to his family and friends. From him we learn that courage is not the absence of fear but rather the doing of what we are afraid to do. Courage allows us to be vulnerable.

No one is courageous all the time, but we all have the capacity for courage if we tap our inner resources. The word *courage* comes from the Latin word for *heart*. It is at the center of our beings—in our hearts—that we discover the marvelous power to live courageously.

Dark Side

*I*f we are ever to be fully alive, we must unveil the dark side of the soul. We will have to admit that we can do evil as well as good and that our nature includes weakness as well as strength, destructiveness as well as creativity.

We are afraid to acknowledge the shadow part of our personalities because then we will no longer be able to maintain the facade of complete goodness. This facade, this mask, is for public consumption. We wear it to get approval from others. We can fool others, and we can even fool ourselves into believing that we are completely good and that evil comes to us from the exterior. We cannot fool God because God knows only too well out of what we are made.

The evil within us does not cease to exist merely because we deny it. The demonic aspects of ourselves cannot be escaped by pretending they are not there. The evil part of the personality is tenacious in its hold on existence and in its desire to be acknowledged and expressed. When we suppress it, we relegate it to the unconscious where it waits patiently until it has an opportunity to break into consciousness. It usually does so in destructive ways at times of crises or inordinate stress.

We are most vulnerable when we believe ourselves to be only pure, clean, and good, and not also soiled, mixed, and evil. When we give evil its due, when we acknowledge it within ourselves, we are in a better position to channel it into more constructive expression in our lives. We can harness the power of evil and turn it to good.

The animal side of our nature has much to offer, if kept in check. From our shadow, which abides in the unconscious, we draw aspects of our humanity essential for abundant living. From the unconscious come spontaneity, creativity, deep and revealing insights, and the ability to express strong emotions. Holding to the one-dimensional nature of the conscious mind in order to receive nods of approval from the world suffocates our free spirit.

To talk about the devil as some kind of metaphysical being "out there" may be a way we project the evil we possess. When we do this, we cannot then wage the struggle with evil where it needs to be waged—within ourselves. By denying evil, we allow it to grow in power and to overtake us from our blind side.

59

The call to wholeness is a call to integrate our conscious and unconscious selves and the good and evil of the personality. From such integration comes a vigorous and life-giving expression of our physical, emotional, intellectual, and spiritual being.

Our life task is not to slay the devil once and for all. Rather, we must face evil constantly within ourselves, knowing that when we have dealt with it we will have to do so again and again. The power of goodness and of evil are both alive and well in us. We make the difference. It is the choice we make on a moment-by-moment basis that tips the scale.

Detachment

*D*etachment seems to run counter to all that we believe about caring for others, yet it is the basis for true love.

Detachment does not mean that we withdraw from others in apathy or that we are not interested in their welfare. It means that we love others enough to let them live their own lives. It also means that we love ourselves enough to mind our own business.

Attachment, on the other hand, forces us to detach from ourselves and to become emotionally overinvolved in the affairs of others. Attachment comes when we believe that we are responsible for the emotions or behavior of others. We play out this illusion by attempting to overtly or covertly control their lives. We become master manipulators in our efforts to influence how others will think, feel, or act. Our attachment appears harmless because we do it in the name of love and we do it "for their own good."

When we are inordinately involved in the lives of others—whether from a parental role or the role of spouse, friend, or caregiver—we tend to obsess and worry. We fill our minds with concerns about others, thus diverting the focus from ourselves.

As we attach, we find ourselves becoming emotionally dependent on others and reacting to them instead of acting from our own center. The more we attach to them, the less we attach to ourselves. The more we try to control them, the less control we have over our own lives.

The more power we give to our obsession with them, the less power we have to take care of ourselves.

We are reluctant to release our attachment because we believe it benefits us. We are afraid to release our attachment because it will appear that we don't care. Perhaps we fear even more that if we detach, we may discover that others can get along very well without our control and overinvolvement in their lives.

We must detach from the life situations of others, not from the persons themselves. We need to detach in order to keep ourselves from becoming enmeshed to the point that we do not know where we end and others begin.

Love compels us to respect the individuality of others and to honor their unique personhood, whether or not we agree with their actions. Through detachment, we can stand back and allow others to be responsible for their own lives, while at the same time protecting ourselves from their behavior. Through

63

detachment, we are better able to defend ourselves because we are not so emotionally entangled. We can set healthy boundaries that will protect us, or we can remove ourselves from the situation altogether if necessary. Above all, through detachment, we move from *reacting* to others to *acting* from the nature of our true selves.

Detachment is hard to do. I would say it is impossible. Yet what is impossible for man and woman is not impossible for God. It is to God that we must turn for the self-love that enables us to detach for our own sake and the sake of others. From God we receive the emotional strength to release others from our grip and to let them be free. From God we gain the courage to abdicate our assumed role as controllers and to focus on what we need to do with our own lives.

Fear

Like a thunderhead looming ominously overhead, our fear moves in to affect our life. The threat of the storm is worse than the storm itself because we cannot fear the present, only that which is to come.

Whether the threat is to our bodies, life-styles, security, loved ones, or to something else, the common thread that runs through all our fears is the possibility of losing someone or something that we hold dear. And the greater the value that we place on our treasure, the greater is our fear of losing it.

As with all emotions, fear is a gift. It is an essential part of our humanity. It is a friend that cautions us about impending danger, a messenger forewarning us. We have been told from early on, however, not to be afraid. We have learned that fear is bad and fearlessness is good. As a result we have spent most of our lives fighting or fleeing fear.

As with any of our emotions, fear will not be ignored. We may deny it, suppress it, or disguise it, but its nature is to do what it must do to get noticed. It will be taken seriously one way or another, even if it has to immobilize us.

The more we fight against our fear, the more it grows out of proportion to reality and the more life and power it gains. The more we run from our fear, the more it overtakes us from within.

What, then, are we to do with fear? How can we let it do the work for which it was intended, to warn us to act or cease acting in order to protect ourselves? First, we must be-friend our fear. Let it be. Don't deny it. Ac-knowledge its significance. What is the danger it warns us of? How tightly are we holding to that which we may lose?

Second, we must not suppress it. Let it have the power it needs, but no more. When we allow our fear to surface, we can face it and experience it fully. Expressing it to another can keep us from denying or suppressing it.

Third, we must not disguise it. We must not put the more socially acceptable mask of anger or sadness on it, because if we can't rec-ognize it, we can't deal with it.

The power of fear is based on illusion—something that is not yet actual. Our imagina-tion works overtime to bolster fear until it be-comes overwhelming. What we fear is in the future, and it frightens us because we believe it is beyond our control, it will happen in a way not of our choosing, and it is un-predictable.

By confronting our fear instead of fighting it, we take away the power it gains from our resistance. We strip it of its mystery and expose its nakedness. We do this by experiencing it fully—by feeling the impact, by not bracing ourselves against it. We diffuse the power of fear by becoming vulnerable to it.

By becoming open to our fear, we are more prepared to take whatever actions are necessary to protect ourselves. By becoming vulnerable to our fear, we become vulnerable to that which we fear. If what we fear is inevitable, then let it happen. Let the storm descend upon us. Let us get tossed and turned, drenched and dirtied. Let us be willing to go through it to the other side. Let us accept the worst that can happen and prepare to deal with it. While we may not control, choose, or predict what will happen to us, we can control, choose, and predict how we will respond to it.

We can respond with love. That is, we can

decide to let go of that which we want most to possess, whether it is a loved one, health, or even life. Instead, through love, we can cling to the essence of God, which we can never lose.

We can respond with faith. We can choose to believe in the power of God and the powerlessness of everything else, even that which we fear. We can choose to believe that while God may not rescue us from the storm, God gives us a mast to cling to and the ability to make it through the tempest.

Focus

*D*uplicity is bondage.
How often we scatter our mental and physical
forces in an attempt to embrace as much as we
can, only to dilute our time, energy, and attention and to end up losing everything.

When we attempt to think of more than
one thing at a time, we become frustrated,
overwhelmed, and confused. When we attempt to move in more than one direction at a
time, we become immobilized. When we attempt to do more than one thing at a time, we

can end up instead doing nothing.

Some of us have the tendency to begin several projects at once and to see none to their completion. Our pride has us believing we can do it all. It is only when we face our real capabilities and limitations, when, through humility, we concentrate on only one project, that we have a chance of accomplishing anything at all.

Perhaps the greatest obstacle to our peace of mind is the temptation to grasp more than one thing at a time. Only a focus and commitment to one thing or one direction will integrate us. We need the faith to let go of all the rest for the time being.

Purity of heart—that is, focus on God and God alone—brings peace to our internal conflict, removes us from the snares of life, and releases us from regulations imposed by the world. Focus frees us from enslavement to external forces and heals us from the internal cancers of ambition, pride, and possessiveness.

Let us spend the rest of our days allowing our hearts to rest in God, allowing our thoughts to be of God. Let us focus our total beings on loving God. Let us help God love us, and the world through us. We must attend constantly to the presence of God by discovering God in all that is.

Forgiveness

Some of us have built impenetrable fortresses from the quarry of an unforgiving nature. With the stones of anger, bitterness, fear, and hate, we have built walls that keep out further injuries and keep in the life-draining memories of past injustices and harms inflicted. Some of us purposely keep open and bleeding the wounds of days gone by.

We will not let go of past hurts because we would have to forgive our transgressors, give up the power we have over them, and let them be free of our control. We are reluctant to release from indebtedness those who have hurt us because we fear it will give them permission to hurt us again. Forgiving them, we think, may suggest we condone their actions or give the impression that we were not, in fact, terribly hurt.

To forgive means "to give." Why should we give anything to those who have hurt us? They don't deserve anything from us except perhaps our wrath.

We must forgive because in doing so we give back to those who hurt us the piece of soul they pawned with us. In the process, we also gain back our own wholeness. If we forgive others, others will often forgive us too. But there is more to it than that. As we forgive, we also release ourselves from the fortress-turned-prison that we have built.

When we forgive those who have injured us in the past, we do not forget the injury or by whom it was inflicted. We need to re-member so that we can protect ourselves from being harmed in the same way. Forgiveness is not tolerance. Our forgiving doesn't mean that we continue to tolerate harm to ourselves. It is important that, as we forgive, we also give no-tice that no more of the same will be tolerated.

Forgiveness does not excuse or ignore the harmful act. It is important that, before we for-give, we confront the perpetrator with the re-ality of the deed. The forgiven one must first be held accountable for his or her actions.

Forgiveness is not just going through the motions. It is more than saying, "I forgive you." Forgiveness is an act of the will. It is freely given, and nothing can be asked in re-turn for it. The forgiven one does not deserve forgiveness and cannot earn it. It is a pure gift to the one forgiven and to the forgiver.

When we forgive, we decide to let go of past hurts. We state it and we mean it from the heart. We don't have to like the person we forgive, but the respect that comes with forgiveness is an element of love.

Forgiveness should not be handed out wholesale, nor should it be taken lightly. It is serious business because it transforms our lives. We will be moved from the moment of pain in which we have been frozen to the present, where we can separate the deed from the doer. We will be freed from the self-imposed chains of reaction, prejudice, and assumption to a place where we can be open to what is now.

As we forgive and let go of past hurts, the walls of our fortress begin to crumble and new life enters, along with new risks and new possibilities for living and loving more abundantly.

Freedom

We are instinctively drawn toward the blissful state of freedom, yet on the path are many counterfeits that lure us into captivity.

Through mid-life, the restraints of life are especially binding and the breaking of all ties seems so appealing. Divorce, quitting a job, leaving the known life behind—all these appear on the horizon as mirages of freedom. Those approaching later life believe that true freedom will come after retirement.

Sometimes it takes us a lifetime of chasing the illusive treasure of freedom to discover that we will never find it by merely changing our exterior life. It is only when we are willing, at any age, to change our interior life that freedom comes.

Freedom is not the lack of boundaries or the absence of responsibility. It is the liberty to choose how we will respond to life from within the state in which we find ourselves, in spite of any limitations imposed on us. Freedom is not doing as we please, but doing what we must to be congruent with our true selves.

Freedom does not come when we declare our independence from parental control, or otherwise overthrow authority. It comes when we silence the voices within that haunt us into subservience and acquiescence.

Freedom is freedom because it doesn't depend upon circumstances to exist. Freedom is a state of maturity in which we accept the power to make choices about our lives. It is the point at which we stop blaming others for our lack of growth and take it upon ourselves to reach our full potential.

Freedom can be bought, but the cost is high. To have it we must be willing to let go of all that matters to us. It will cost us our sense of security, power, pride, prestige, and control. It will even cost us our sense of freedom.

Freedom comes when we hitch our wagon to the power of the trust within us—when, through consciousness of the God within, we focus, not on our will, but on God's, not on our life, but on God's life in us.

Goodbye

We live and love, but then we must say goodbye.

Why is it that when we most want to hold on to what we have, it is taken from our grasp? Why can't something be forever? Why must we always say goodbye? Even from the beginning, that which was important to us was lost when we most wanted it.

From the security of our mothers' arms we were expelled, in order that we could explore the world. We may have inherited the world, but we never quite got over what we had to leave behind.

Even as we enjoyed the haven of our youth, when time itself seemed to stand still, we were abruptly cast out to confront the rest of life. We received adulthood and the task of serious living, but even now we look back to a place and time that will never come our way again.

Remember those special friends with whom we shared so much? Our friendships would be forever, we vowed; and then the friends were gone, and our hearts were broken. Memory sustains us, but to our friends we had to say goodbye.

As we grew older, we came to learn that even dreams and plans must sometimes go. Once they were our motivation, purpose, and direction, but with the passing of time they dissipated along with possibilities, and we had to say goodbye.

For so long we held to expectations of

what should be. Our marriages and families would be just so. Our jobs would be fulfilling and rewarding. Our lives would be abundant.

As we lived, we came to know that our expectations and life's realities were not to be the same. The storybook lives we created didn't last long. People changed, we changed, and circumstances around us changed. We could not hold on to that which was. As we adjusted to what was real, we had to say goodbye to our ideal.

The accidents of life have also robbed us of what we've held so dear. Out of nowhere have come those crucifying moments when we have lost a loved one through death or separation or have lost our health or even our way of life.

Because these have been accidents, they have done violence to our life and have turned us inside out. In the process we have grieved what we have lost, and then we have had to say goodbye.

In our woundedness and vulnerability, we hesitate to live and love again. For a while, we refuse to embrace anything or anyone lest we be forced again to say goodbye.

As we begin to heal we venture out in life. We dare once more to dream, to risk, to invest, and to love.

Perhaps it is only spiritual life to which we can cling. For it is when we say goodbye to the actual that we can say hello to the spiritual. When we release what has been ours, it takes on a different nature. We may no longer hold it in our hands, but we can hold it in our hearts. We may no longer live it, but we can forever be mindful of it.

The paradox is that by letting go of what we love, it is ours to have forever more. It seems that the integration of total life comes only when we have allowed the disintegration of its parts. It is because we say goodbye to what we love that it becomes a part of memory, a part of who we are.

Grief

*T*he major losses that we suffer in life seem like mountains that cannot be transcended. Their shadow is cast upon us and we are overwhelmed with devastating grief. We have climbed the peaks of life before and we have walked into its valleys, but these mountains seem too high, too wide—impassable. The only way to the other side of the mountains is through the tunnel and, unless we enter its darkness, we will never see the light again.

Loss hurts and we are tempted to pretend that it hasn't happened or, having happened, that it doesn't really affect. But it does.

Unresolved grief is one of the major causes of dysfunctional lives, and yet it is not something to which we give much attention. We are constantly suffering losses large and small, and each of them needs to be acknowledged and dealt with honestly and completely.

The little deaths are the ones that can be ignored the easiest and the longest and that can do us the most damage. It may be the loss of a job that we must grieve, the end of a relationship, the letting go of an expectation, the saying goodbye to a former way of life—including a bad habit—or just the recognition that nothing stays the same or lasts forever. But grieve we must, lest the loss fester within us and infect us with the disease of unresolved melancholy.

We have no choice but to enter the belly of the whale and stay there long enough to be transformed by pain, and then to surface with new breath and new life.

One way we avoid the pain of loss is to deny the loss itself. We may behave as though a loved one really hasn't died, a marriage or significant relationship isn't over, or a sudden loss of health has not occurred. But deep inside we know the truth, and the incongruency deprives us of wholeness and wellness.

Another way we deny is by acknowledging the loss but suppressing the feelings of sorrow and grief that normally accompany loss. Some of us put our emotions on hold, hoping that they will go away or at least diminish in intensity. But the more feelings are denied or suppressed, the more they intensify and the greater their need to be expressed. And they will be expressed, if not appropriately and constructively, then inappropriately and destructively.

Yet another way we deny the grief of loss is by using our religion to sugar coat the bitterness of life. A faith that denies reality is not faith but delusion. We must not substitute religion for the task of grief that faces us after a significant loss. Our religion must be based on the reality of life; life is change, and change is a series of deaths and resurrections.

Those who are willing to be real, who are daring enough to be human and confront the suffering that comes with living and losing, will not be abandoned. They will receive the strength they need to sustain loss, endure pain, and transcend grief.

God suffers with us through profound compassion. Our heartache is God's heartache, our tears are God's tears, our journey through the tunnel of grief is one we make with God. With God we love and live, with God we lose and die, with God we love and live again.

Grieving What
Never Was

*E*ven that which was
lost to us from the beginning—that which was
never ours to lose—must be grieved as we
journey toward wholeness.

It has been said that what we never had
we never miss, but experience shows us that
this is not the case with those things that are
basic to our human development. There are
basic needs that all of us have, and when those
needs have not been met, we are left with gaping holes in our souls.

We can pretend that those holes do not exist by stuffing them with drugs, alcohol, work, unhealthy relationships, or other addictions that we believe will anesthetize us against the pain and emptiness we feel. Or we can look honestly and courageously into those holes and discover what it is that has been missing from the start. Once we realize and acknowledge what was never ours, we must allow ourselves to grieve it as though it had been ours and had somehow been lost.

Some of us may discover that we have never had the security we needed as a foundation for life. If we came from homes in which each day was unpredictable and full of turmoil, or homes in which we were physically, sexually, or emotionally abused, we lived in an unsafe world. We may have grown up cautious, suspicious, and guarded. We may have become people who seek control in every situation in order to feel safe. It is important to grieve the loss of the security we never had and to seek it anew from within.

Others of us may realize that we never experienced the freedom to be ourselves. If we were raised by overprotective parents or parents who were domineering or authoritarian, we were denied the latitude to make mistakes and to learn from the consequences of our actions. Now we may be afraid to make decisions or to survive on our own. Restricted and confined, we long for the freedom that we never knew. This freedom must be grieved, and new freedom must be found by breaking free from the chains of the past.

Some of us didn't have a father or a mother, either because they were dead or because they were physically and emotionally absent from us. It is sad as adults to realize we didn't get that vital connection with a father or a mother when we needed it most. We need to grieve the father or the mother that we never had, and we need to discover deep within the parental support that we can give ourselves.

93

Some of us were forced by the nature of our family life to give up childhood even as we entered it. We may have been compelled to take on adulthood before our time. We may have been thrust into the role of surrogate spouse or surrogate parent, or we may have been cast into the role of peacemaker or problem-solver. Whatever major responsibility we took on as children cheated us out of a carefree and joy-filled childhood.

What about love itself? We may discover that we were never really loved except conditionally and manipulatively. If we have a hard time loving others without trying to control them, it may be because we were never loved unconditionally. We must grieve what might have been and then release it to the past. Now it is up to us to love ourselves with the unconditional love of God.

Even as adults we lose what we have never had. Miscarriages and abortions are often not grieved because there was never a

94

birth; yet, something was lost even before it was gained, and that something must be grieved.

Dreams that were never realized and plans that were never executed must be grieved. Marriages that never happened and education that was never obtained must be grieved. Professional rank that was never attained and feats that were never accomplished must be grieved.

Grieving what never was helps us face up to the reality of what is. It helps us feel the emotions that naturally follow the loss of something valued. It helps us come to grips with life without all that we wanted, and it helps us invest in something new that we can have.

Growth

It is one thing to talk about growth and quite another to actually enter into it. We would rather flee from the disconcerting experience growth puts us through. We fear the pain that growth necessitates, and we cling tenaciously to that which growth would have us release.

Go away, growth! We will have nothing to do with you. You come and disturb the status quo in which we are comfortably stuck. You expose the dead limbs on our tree of life, and

97

you prune them mercilessly. We cannot bear
the pain of loss, even of that which is dead or
detrimental to the whole. And yet, if we
choose life, we must choose growth, for it is
the only way to stay alive, the only path toward wholeness.

It is no wonder we are frightened by
growth. It comes as a death-and-resurrection
experience. To grow we must cross over from
a seemingly safe place to one that is unknown,
toward which we must stretch. Growth brings
with it a disintegration of the old and a separation from former ways. Growth means painful
transition that includes periods in limbo, when
we are neither in the old nor in the new. And
finally, growth brings integration based on a
new consciousness of who we are and who we
need to become.

But what price, this becoming? What does
growth require of us? First, there must be a
commitment to wholeness. Not a passive allowing of growth, but a definite yes to the op-

portunity to become all we can be. Then we must be willing to confront those aspects of ourselves that we have avoided and claim ownership of those traits that block effective living.

We are burdened by old habits that stunt our growth and dysfunctional patterns that work against us and others. They are deeply ingrained in our way of life, yet they must be uprooted to make way for healthy habits and life-giving patterns. This does not happen all at once; becoming takes a lifetime.

What else does growth ask of us? It would have us admit our mistakes and grow from them instead of stubbornly defending our illusion of perfection. Growth also would have us become more aware of our emotions, for they are the voice of the psyche. We need to listen and learn from them. Our feelings help us to become real, if we acknowledge them and express them.

The more real, the more authentic we be-

come, the more spiritually aware we will be.
We stop being controlled by the effort to pre-
serve our image and the favorable opinion of
others, and begin to listen to the inner voice
that moves us toward what we need to be
about. The more authentic we become, the
fewer games we will allow ourselves to play
and the more genuine our relationships will
be.

We need perseverance in our growth, for
we are easily distracted from the task and
quickly tempted to give up the difficult struggle. And we need the courage to continue
even in the face of fear, working one moment
at a time.

Growth would have us be disciplined in
our routines and techniques for living. This
must not be the discipline of an obedient sol-
dier or an acquiescent son or daughter, but the
discipline of the soul responding to a higher
calling. It will mean making daily choices that
promote growth, such as the choices to pray

and meditate, rest and exercise, read and write, participate and abstain.

Growth will have us develop those parts of ourselves that are undeveloped and use to the fullest those parts that have been our strengths. It will have us enhance our consciousness through open interaction with others and explore our unconscious through the inner work that we must do.

We may enter into growth kicking and screaming, and agonize in the process; yet, in the end, we will rejoice at having surrendered to the potential of our humanity.

Heroism

The hero we seek we will find within ourselves. Many of us spend our lives searching for someone to admire, respect, and emulate. We attribute great qualities to entertainers, athletes, politicians, and other public persons in the hope that they will match our standards for heroism and meet our need to look up to someone with awe and inspiration.

We are often disappointed upon learning that our heroes and heroines are not above and beyond the norm after all, that they have weaknesses just like everyone else.

We become disillusioned and cynical about the higher good that we want to experience vicariously. Before long, however, we have identified another candidate for heroism, and we begin to invest in the illusion once again.

Technology and rapid change have left many of us feeling relatively useless, our roles in life seeming superfluous. We no longer confront life as a challenge, but merely cope with it to get by.

No wonder we look to the heroic deeds of fictional characters to fantasize our own heroism. Our hero worship is an external sign of our internal emptiness.

We have abdicated our own heroic roles in the name of comfort, desire, and apathy. We have stopped being heroes and heroines because of fear, compulsions, and a disconnectedness with our spiritual selves. Our abdication is due in part to the way we define heroism. Some of us see heroes as being perfect, fearless, and strong. When, in our humanity, we realize that we are none of these, we let others to whom we attribute these traits be our heroes and heroines.

Heroism is the willingness to go beyond the established boundaries of the self and to reach for the higher good in the world and in ourselves, despite our imperfections, fears, and weaknesses.

Sacrifice is not tantamount to heroism, but when we make sacrifices to attain the higher good, that is heroic. Heroism includes deeds, to be sure, but it is not limited to deeds. To overcome adversity is heroic. To make the best of bad and inevitable circumstances is heroic. To be willing to enter into therapy or treatment in order to change dysfunctional behavior or crippling addiction is heroic. To remain open to all that life gives us, including loss and growth, death and resurrection, is heroic.

Our lives are full of opportunities for heroism. At every turn we are challenged to be all that we can be. It is in reaching for this potential that we become heroes and heroines.

The disease, poverty, war, and injustice that plague our world and our immediate community are the arenas in which we must do the best we can to alleviate problems. Closer to home, we must confront our own psychological disease, poverty of spirit, warring internal factions, and propensity toward injustice.

To be willing to transform a stable and stagnant existence to one in which we take responsibility for ourselves and our world is the stuff of heroes and heroines. Heroism is the intellectual, emotional, physical, and spiritual explosion that happens in us when we allow ourselves to be fully human and alive. Heroism is the courage with which we respond to our calling as sons and daughters of God.

Heroism is the force within us that God uses to affect the world according to God's loving will. We are all instruments of God. We are all heroes and heroines.

Humiliation

We know no poverty like the loss of our dignity. To have our sense of self-respect ripped away from us is an experience we remember forever. Humiliation can be so emotionally painful that we would rather endure its equivalent—or more—in physical pain. When we are humiliated early in life, we develop a tremendous fear that it may happen to us again. The impact of humiliation is long-lasting and pervasive, and it hovers over us like a dark and dreaded cloud.

Our humiliation may have consisted of extreme embarrassment. We may have been humiliated in childhood by a clumsy parent who scolded us in front of company or disregarded our need for privacy. We may have been humiliated by an insensitive teacher who shamed us in front of the entire class. We may have been humiliated by nasty schoolmates who ridiculed us or made fun of us. We may have been humiliated by ourselves, that is, by something we did to look foolish in front of others.

For some of us, the experience of humiliation was even more painful. This is especially true for those who were physically, sexually, or emotionally abused. Only those to whom such abuse has happened can understand the sense of powerlessness, emptiness, and nakedness one is left to deal with for the rest of one's life. Always there is the fear that it may happen again. Always there is the vigilance that keeps life in a virtual state of suspension.

Humiliation afflicts us so deeply because it touches the core of our being. To be humiliated is to be stripped of respect, integrity, and selfhood. It cuts deep into the fiber of our identity and leaves us with an open wound.

Those of us who have suffered humiliation in one way or another have made a conscious decision to avoid the recurrence of such an experience at any cost. The way we have done so is through excessive control over our environment. Our control has focused especially on stifling our emotions, curtailing spontaneity lest we be caught off guard, and managing our image so that others see only those parts of us that we consider acceptable.

It is not humiliation that is so destructive to us in adulthood, but rather the fear of it. We are not afraid so much of the actual moment of humiliation—for we can survive that somehow—but of what might happen as a result of our tarnished image. We fear the loss of respect from others. We fear the loss of their esteem. We are afraid that others will not like us or love us if they see us at our worst. We are afraid of rejection and abandonment. We are prisoners of our fear.

There are those who have been set free from the prison of fear; they stand as a model for the rest of us. They have transcended their fear of humiliation by confronting it. Through repeated experiences of humiliation, they have conquered the fear. It is not that they are comfortable being humiliated, but that now they have attached themselves to something they deem more important than looking good to others. Humiliation still hurts, but they know that it hurts even more to be less that fully alive. They have found an internal peace based on unconditional love for themselves, regardless of how they look to others.

We too can release the control we have over our image. We can face the worst and survive as long as we attach ourselves to something more important than how others see us. This something is the knowledge that God is within us and will remain with us no matter what we do or how we look. We can come to believe that we will be all right as long as we cling to the one who will never ridicule us, never abandon us, and never stop loving us. Knowing this, we can handle the rest courageously. Let us give up trying to protect our image in the world and focus instead on how we are known by God.

Intimacy

We can bestow no greater gift on one another than to confess the secret of who we are and what we are about. Intimacy is a need inherent in our humanity; it is the need to be real and to be accepted, validated, and understood by another as we are.

Without this acceptance, there can be no true union between two persons. Too often, however, it is assumed that intimacy should be easily forthcoming. Others demand that we disclose our deepest nature and our most private self. But intimacy is not to be presupposed as part of any relationship, including marriage. Rather, intimacy grows like a wild flower when the conditions are right for it to sink its roots and spread its petals.

Intimacy can grow only where the soil is free of the choking weeds of criticism and judgment. It flourishes where the raindrops of encouragement nourish it and the sunlight of understanding invites its presence.

The quest for intimacy must take into account our fear of self-disclosure, which may be rooted in childhood. As children we may have been told that feelings were not to be expressed. We may have been victims of extensive emotional abuse, including constant criticism. As a result, we may have learned that the best defense was to keep to ourselves and disclose nothing that might be used against us.

It may be that in the past our willingness to be intimate was used to manipulate or control us, and we are now afraid to disclose ourselves.

There is within each of us a core which only God can penetrate. There is a self within us that only God can know. This most intimate self is not to be disturbed. We are right to protect this center against all possible invasion. Yet, there is so much of our private self that can be known to one who earns our trust. There is a whole world of our interior self that can be shared with one who lets us be.

The fragile nature of intimacy must never be forgotten. It cannot be pushed and pulled by the forces of expectation. It cannot be tossed and turned by the waves of disrespect.

The demand for intimacy must be silenced, and in its place must come a love that is open and a will that sets us free. Slowly and steadily we take the risk in this safer environment, and our risk is rewarded with acceptance. Trust opens the door and intimacy ventures out. We dare to share our essential self, we come closer than ever before, we make contact, and we move into the realm of the familiar. The intimacy that grows between two persons is the gift of love.

Letting Go

The life we live is but a thousand deaths, and it is our willingness to go through these deaths that is the hope of our life.

Death has many faces, but always it is the prerequisite to abundant living. Yet it is so hard to die. We are frightened by death's shadows and blinded by its darkness. Only by faith can we let go unto death, that we may live.

Finis in Latin means both *end* and *goal*. This

is the way of life: endings and beginnings, deaths and resurrections. Our task is to let endings be endings, in order that we may set new goals. For without setting new goals, we slide into despair. Endings and goals depend on one another.

In letting go of what would be, we embrace what is, no matter how painful. In living reality, we will experience more peace than in any glorious fantasy we can imagine. When we attempt to escape from the actual to avoid suffering, we end up suffering more because we are separated from ourselves, and that is hell.

The death that comes is the letting go of the security that the world offers. In the wake of that death comes the discovery that the only true security lies within the soul. The death that comes releases others to be who they can be and releases us to find new roles and new adventures in living.

When we lock ourselves into expectations,

we lock out openness to what will come. Expectations kill the patience, tolerance, and spontaneity that bring us peace.

In our life there will be yearnings that we will not fill. The fulfillment of peace will depend on our acceptance of those unfulfilled yearnings.

We sometimes believe that holding on to old resentments is what keeps us alive. The opposite is true. It is only when we are willing to deal with stored-up emotions that we can lay them to rest and allow new life to flow through us. With the death of old debts comes the life of new freedom.

The dark places of our past keep us sick and lacking in peace. The healing of those hurtful memories comes only through shedding light on them, so that we may see their influence on us.

Some deaths come unexpectedly and unsolicited. Others we bring about. Such is the case with harmful addictions, whether to habits, substances, or persons. Here, it is not a matter of allowing the death to take place or dealing a deathblow to our addiction. Rather, it has to do with believing in a higher life, a better way. As we give a place in our life to a higher power, the lower power fades into death.

This is the paradox of life. Only through disintegration of that which is not life-giving do we become integrated into a life that is vital, meaningful, and eternal.

Loneliness

*L*oneliness can be a cornerstone of our self-actualization or a boulder that crushes our lives. Loneliness is an inherent part of the human condition. Our self-awareness predisposes us to loneliness. Each of us decides what to do with our loneliness, and our response to it becomes our religion, our daily life.

Our loneliness begins when we become conscious of separation from our mother at birth and doesn't end until we enter unity through death. It is a natural part of life and touches all of us.

The feeling of loneliness is sometimes confused with other emotions. Although loneliness may produce depression, they are not the same. Neither is loneliness nostalgia or melancholia. Loneliness is an emotional isolation in which we become painfully aware that something is missing in life.

Loneliness is the acute and painful awareness of our separation, and it may be prompted by different experiences. We may miss a special person, we may feel alienated from God, we may approach a significant event such as a holiday or anniversary alone, or we may feel neglected by the world.

Being with others does not by itself alleviate the sense of loneliness. We can feel lonely in the midst of a crowd, and we can experience no loneliness when we are alone.

We may discover much loneliness in a family that appears to be radiant with community atmosphere but in which there is little or no communication going on. A widow or widower may look with envy at a married person who appears fulfilled, not suspecting that the married person returns each day to the loneliness of an empty marriage.

We do not want to experience loneliness. We have a dreadful fear of it. This fear has us evading, denying, and otherwise escaping our loneliness. Our attempt to escape brings on even more loneliness. We overeat, watch television excessively, work ourselves into the ground, remain constantly active, spend money, seek out crowds, or turn to alcohol and other drugs. But all is in vain. Sometimes we attempt to overcome loneliness by giving up our individuality and becoming dependent on another. This only works against us. The pain of loneliness, which can be more severe than physical pain, will not be relieved through obsessive, compulsive behavior.

Only by courageously facing inevitable

loneliness can we convert it to new and fruitful life. When we face loneliness openly and live with it honestly, we begin to develop our inner resources. By allowing ourselves to experience not the fear of loneliness but loneliness itself, we become more compassionate toward others, dare to risk intimate relationships, and grow emotionally and spiritually. Our loneliness tells us of our incompleteness and moves us toward wholeness. Through the experience of loneliness, we are brought more deeply in touch with the true nature of our existence.

Although faith is not a cure for loneliness, it gives us a framework in which to better understand and deal with it. Our belief must not be that we will be saved from loneliness but that something can always be done about and with our loneliness. To begin, we can stop making others responsible for our loneliness. Waiting to be rescued by others will only lead to more pain. When we take it upon ourselves to risk loving, our own need to be loved will be fulfilled and our loneliness will be diminished.

Friendship, the source of nourishment we need so desperately, comes as a result of reaching out toward others. It is an active and enthusiastic participation that will move us from loneliness to new life. Loneliness cannot be chased away by frantic activity, but it fades in the light of our individual and unique purpose in life.

There is a point beyond which no one can accompany us, even through empathy. The compassion, comfort, and companionship of others may see us through many grave moments of our life, yet the moment of our passion is a moment spent alone. We must then bear the pain without the support, strength, and presence of others. In the midst of our fear and anguish, we reach out and no one is there.

It is at these times of existential loneliness that we feel abandoned, empty, and vulnerable to the wolves. There is no place to turn but within, to the secret place of the soul.

Having let go of our reliance on things of the world to protect us, having released even our loved ones as our saviors, we come to discover the one and only source of our security. We come to know the God who will never leave us alone because we are a part of God.

This basic human loneliness, which cannot be relieved even by those who love us most, is the condition that turns us back to God. It is a thirst that can be quenched only at God's fountain.

Love of Self

Love of self is the seed of holistic living. It is sown deep in the soul, if and when we are willing to receive it, by an unconditionally loving God. For the most part, we are not willing to receive it because we believe that self-love is narcissistic, selfish, and self-centered.

Many of us believe that self-love takes away from the love we have for others. Actually, the more we are able to love ourselves, the more we are able to love others. Love of self is the Golden Rule in reverse: we need to do unto ourselves as we would do unto others.

As we are aware of the needs of others, we need to be aware of our own needs. As we give nurturing, support, and encouragement to others, we need to give the same to ourselves. As we accept others with all their good and bad traits, we also need to accept ourselves unconditionally.

This is the first step to self-love: to accept ourselves as we are, not judging, criticizing, or shaming, but only accepting. This does not mean that we are to be complacent. Rather, we allow ourselves to grow in an atmosphere of personal affirmation.

To love ourselves means that we can see the reality of who we are and encourage ourselves to change where change is necessary. At the same time, we also need to compliment ourselves for what we know to be good about us, and we need to acknowledge and accept the compliments that others give us.

Love includes taking care of ourselves physically. The body is a masterpiece of function that must be attended to with dedication. We need to listen to it and respond to what it tells us. This means resting when we are tired, taking a break when we are burned out, and stopping harmful habits. Loving ourselves physically means that we feed ourselves properly, exercise appropriately, and sleep adequately. We do not do this through deprivation, pressure, or guilt, but as a result of a sincere concern for our own welfare.

Love of self means developing the mind. We need to pursue our interests. We learn not only from books, but also from entering into the exciting experience of life. We love ourselves when we continually open ourselves to different persons and places and enter into dialogue with the world.

We love ourselves emotionally when we allow our feelings to be known to ourselves and others. Sharing our emotional selves with others whom we trust is self-loving, as is emotional intimacy with a special person.

To love ourselves we must first accept the unconditional love of God. This requires a close relationship with God through prayer. Love of self will compel us to leave the crowd and venture into solitude with God. Here we gain the acceptance that restores the soul.

From God's unconditional acceptance comes the capacity to forgive, respect, trust, and honor ourselves. From God's total love for us comes the self-love that relieves us of the guilt we may have carried for years.

Self-love allows us to ask for help from others when we need it and to accept nurturing and support from those who love us. From self-love comes the responsibility to defend ourselves against any form of abuse, including ways we abuse ourselves, and to say no, when necessary, to the demands of others. Self-love enables us to reach for the child with-

in us, to have fun, and to enjoy life to the fullest.

Loving ourselves means that we become
aware of our personal dignity as created beings of God. It means that we allow ourselves
to experience a sense of worthiness, not for
what we do, but simply for who we are. Loving ourselves means that we come to believe
in ourselves and our ability to fulfill the mission of love in the world.

Making Amends

*I*f we are estranged
from others, we are not whole. We are called
by love to reconcile with our brother or sister
whom we have harmed. To reconcile may
mean to restore the relationship by bringing a
sense of harmony back to it, to settle or resolve
a conflict, or to simply accept and be willing to
work with the disagreement.

The first step in reconciliation is to recall
that your brother or sister has something
against you. That is, we must inventory our

lives and bring to mind the damage we have done to others, whether physical, psychological, or spiritual. To remember the ways we may have been unjust, ungrateful, uncaring, unresponsive, or unloving will move us to compunction. To recall the nature of our role in the suffering of others will help us see how the connection was severed.

It is not enough to be sorry for our actions or inactions. Whenever possible, we must act to counterbalance the harm we have done. When we recall specific ways we have violated others, we will be better able to decide how to make our amends.

As we repent for what we have done or failed to do, we search for ways we can atone for our mistakes. Atonement implies some kind of reparation for the offense or injury to others. It is an act through which we are "at-one" with them again.

If we have harmed another through neglect, our presence and attention will be our amends. If we have lied to them, truth will be the order of the day. If we have been apathetic to the plight of others, active concern may be called for. Our amends may be simply to stop a harmful behavior.

If we have hurt someone to whom, because of circumstances, we can no longer make direct amends, we can atone indirectly through our interaction with others. When we cannot regain what we have lost or repair what we have damaged, we do well to seek restoration in symbolic ways.

We may never even the score, but that is not the idea anyway. What matters is our attitude toward the way we have lived in the past and the way we want to live now and in the future.

Making amends to those whom we have harmed involves a change of heart and a change of behavior. We undergo a transformation. As we are reconciled with our brother or sister, whether directly or indirectly, we are also reconciled with ourselves.

Masks

*L*et us know the peace that comes from being real.

Watch the little child as she plays, cries, or cuddles in your arms. She wears no mask. She does not pretend to be more or less than she is. She dares to be herself. She knows the peace that comes from congruence between her inner and outer selves. Yet soon she will learn about masks. She will begin to react to her environment just as we did when we were growing up. She will adjust to the expectations of society by covering up her true self with masks that are more acceptable to the world.

One's mask, what is sometimes called the persona, is the image one gives to the world. It is a facade that conceals the true self, including one's real thoughts and feelings. The mask or persona is a compromise that an individual makes with society as to what a person should appear to be, a compromise between the demands of the environment and the inner needs of the individual. The mask includes not only the way one thinks, but also the way one behaves, dresses, gestures, walks, and talks.

Each of us develops this mask because we need it to deal with the world. It can be inappropriate and sometimes dangerous to expose our inner selves. Our masks can protect us from unnecessary vulnerability. They can serve as barriers between our more delicate inner selves and the demanding outer world. They work against us, however, when we begin to wear them all the time, or when we are taken in by them ourselves.

We lose touch with reality when we begin to identify with the masks we wear. Much like an actor who begins to believe he really is the character he plays on stage, we lose sense of the difference between who we are and who we pretend to be.

The masks we wear are formed in reaction to our life experiences. When expectations at home or school are imposed in such a way that we feel rejected unless we acquiesce, it is easy to see why we pretend to be who others want us to be. Perhaps it was a parent who we could never please, one who expected us to be perfect. The mask we chose to wear may have been that of the clown who laughs on the outside and cries on the inside.

Maybe the environment to which we reacted was one of inordinate strictness or oppression. To survive we may have chosen the masks of seriousness, soldier-like discipline, or task orientation. If our childhood environment was filled with chaos, confusion, insecurity, and unpredictability, we may have chosen the mask of excessive control over ourselves and our environment.

Whatever our personal experiences, the result was that we decided early on to take the path of least resistance, and since then we have neglected our real selves behind the masks. When we lose touch with our real selves, we also lose peace of mind because we use a tremendous amount of energy and suffer a great deal of stress pretending to be who we are not.

To live life in total compliance with the expectations of society is to become a compromised, conformed, mass person. On the other hand, to live without regard for the environment is to live as an eccentric or misfit. The balance that must be struck is based on a constant awareness that the masks we use to adapt to the world are not the same as our identity. To be well-adjusted in life is to understand the purpose of masks and to use them when appropriate without losing touch with our true selves.

The more we tend to the unfinished business of our past lives, the more we look to ourselves rather than others for the approval and acceptance we need. The more we live according to our true selves, the less we will be tempted to use masks to face the world.

Perhaps we never set aside our masks permanently. Perhaps we never completely trust the world around us. But more and more, as we dare to take off those masks and risk being ourselves—regardless of who that might be—we bring about a congruence that results in personal peace.

Peace

*F*or everything we desire in life, we must give up something else. What is the price we are willing to pay for peace?

Some of us say we want to run to a desert island, leaving behind all our worries and tribulations. But we cannot find peace by running away from life. Others of us are willing to let the world have its way with us. We acquiesce to the demands and manipulations of others in order to avoid conflict and confrontation. But avoidance of trouble does not result in peace. Others of us seek peace by altering the external circumstances of our lives, yet even this will not bring us peace.

Where, then, can we find peace? The source of our peace lies within. It is there for us to tap, regardless of life circumstances. Peace comes from within or not at all.

We are so used to going after what we want that even peace becomes a quest for us. We are surprised to discover that peace comes, not as a result of what we can get hold of, but as a result of letting go. Letting go of what? Of the illusion that we control our lives or the lives of others. Certainly, we make decisions and choices about what we will or will not do, but in the final analysis we are not in control of what is to happen. If we can learn to get out of our own way, we have a chance at peace. Our efforts do violence to the peace that would be ours if only we would let go of our preoccupation with ourselves.

Peace is not contingent on the ease with which we live, and it has little to do with peaceful circumstances. Peace has everything to do with how we respond to the moment before us. We can either charge into it with our own willpower and self-confidence or let go and depend on a power beyond us that brings all things to good.

Peace does not come with the removal of external problems, but with the internal awareness that we are not alone as we face them. With God in us, we can cope with whatever comes our way.

The absence of anxiety and fear is not peace. An easy and harmless life is not peace. Peace is ours in the midst of trouble. It overcomes us amid chaos and indecision when we realize that we are in the care of God. Peace comes when we recognize the hand that holds ours, even in the darkness. Peace is knowing in the depths of the soul that we are not alone. The eternal is with us always.

Peace comes to us when we place our hope beyond ourselves, our limitations, and our helplessness. Peace comes from union with God. To let God live through us is to do God's will, and to do God's will is to live in peace.

Perfection

The perfection toward which we strive is a mirage in the desert of life. We will never arrive at it, but in our obsession with it we miss what can give us life—God's unconditional love and acceptance of us just as we are.

From God's love for us comes the love we have for ourselves, and self-love means that we allow ourselves to be in process. We embrace our faults as well as our gifts, our strengths as well as our weaknesses. To be perfect in this way is to be tolerant of our in-completeness.

God's perfection is manifested in the full-ness of God's redeeming love for us. It is this integrating love and all-encompassing ac-ceptance that we are to emulate.

The dictionary defines *perfectionism* as a "disposition to regard anything short of per-fection as unacceptable." This is the attitude many of us have taken toward ourselves. We have wasted much of life chasing an illusion, to our detriment and that of those around us.

For some of us perfectionism is deeply in-grained in our personality from early child-hood conditioning. Some perfectionists never experienced a sense of approval from their parents. They only heard about their short-comings. Some were constantly attacked through criticism, ridicule, or control. Their ability was doubted by those in whom they believed all power and knowledge resided.

The tragedy is that some perfectionists believe their apparent imperfections make them unlovable. They have spent their lives striving to overcome the imperfect image that was imposed on them, trying at every turn to be perfect. They believe that if only they can achieve perfection, they will receive the respect, love, and acceptance they didn't get before.

As children, perfectionists were focused on pleasing their disapproving parents. They adopted their parents' unrealistic standards and took them into adulthood. Now their overriding concern is to please the critical parents in their heads.

Perfectionists want to feel good about themselves, but they only allow this to happen when they experience a sense of perfection. Since this is rarely possible for any of us, their usual attitude is one of guilt and worthlessness.

Perfectionists are extremists. For them, a small event can become a catastrophe. Perfectionists tend to exaggerate a small mistake into a disappointment of major consequences.

When we do not accept ourselves because of our perfectionism, we also have trouble accepting others. We become impatient with and critical of those around us; our frustration with ourselves spills onto them.

When we expect perfection from ourselves or others, we build walls of unreality that block intimacy from developing, for intimacy comes from unconditional acceptance between two persons. The quickest way to put up barriers between oneself and another is to impose "shoulds" and "oughts" on the other.

Perfectionism is hard work. It takes away all the energy we have, and it gets us absolutely nowhere. What *will* work for us is progress, not perfectionism. All we need to do is keep moving forward (allowing for a backward step from time to time). We need to be content to work at it, all the while accepting ourselves completely, imperfections and all.

Rather than inspire or encourage us toward better living, unrealistic expectations keep us feeling inadequate and defeated. When we establish realistic standards and goals for ourselves, we are encouraged, motivated, and elevated toward higher self-esteem.

To be whole is to be willing to accept an imperfect world that is populated by imperfect beings. When we embrace the world as it is, we can work to make it better. When we embrace ourselves as we are, we can begin to grow. When we embrace others as they are, they can begin to accept themselves. This is the way of love.

Perspective

*T*rouble lurks in the shadows of night, and the world seems an ugly place to be. But do not be dismayed; things will look different in the morning light.

Whether it is new light shed on the circumstances or the same light observed from a different angle, our perspective on something can change from night to day.

Perhaps we are mired in the bustle and chaos of the marketplace of life, feeling confused and overstimulated. Yet, if we gave ourselves a little distance and took a short climb up a nearby hill, we could gain a new look at where we have been. Our overview might help us to understand the whole of which we are a part. We might even return with a different attitude.

We may be feeling overwhelmed by responsibilities and fearful of undertaking what seem to be formidable tasks. Yet, if we broke down each job into distinct and individual parts to be handled one at a time, we could produce a less intimidating picture and allay our fears.

We may be faced with family problems, physical ailments, or a general malaise about life. Things may seem dim and hopeless. Yet, if we removed ourselves from the midst of our circumstances and considered alternative measures to deal with our plight, we could be empowered to gain some control over our lives.

How we look at something determines

what meanings we give to it and, consequently, how we respond to it. It is within our power to change how we perceive a given circumstance and therefore to change our behavior toward it.

Sometimes changing our perspective requires that we stand back and view the larger picture. Sometimes it means that we must come closer and take a careful look at the intricacies in order to understand more fully. Sometimes all we need to do is change our position, and we begin to see things we have not seen before.

It is helpful for us to periodically move from our traditional and comfortable place and to approach from a new angle. We can read a book or an article written by someone with whom we adamantly disagree. We can put ourselves in the place of a child or another adult to see how they would perceive things. Role reversal can be a healthy way to see the other side.

To see things only from one point of view stifles us and keeps us stuck in our constricted prejudices. To change our vantage point and give different meaning to what we see is to open ourselves to a treasure chest of new possibilities. Putting an old perspective in a new frame enables us to expand the reaches of our mind and gain new energy with which to respond to life.

Whether new insight comes to us as a result of a trip around the world or just across the street, it enhances life. Whether we see things more clearly from an orbiting spaceship or from atop a tree in our backyard, we are richer for it.

To gain a new and different perspective by changing how we look at things does not come without resistance. We are afraid to let go of our old perspectives. We are afraid of change and of what change will require of us. We are afraid to admit we may have been wrong.

The price of new awareness is detachment from old awareness. We cannot receive new consciousness if fear is entrenched in our minds. The courage required to detach and move from one vantage point to another comes from the faith we have in a God who reveals great secrets to us. The ability to reframe events and circumstances is the tool God gives us to overcome the difficulties of life, no matter how dark things may seem.

Play

*P*lay is the refreshment of the soul. It is more than important in our lives; it is vital. Play is a means through which we can be re-created, a way to become fully human.

"But I don't have time to play," we may say. "There are too many demands on me, too much to do. How can you talk about playing when living is such serious business?" It is precisely because life is filled with so much that is serious that we are called to play. We are playful by nature, but we have become conditioned to set aside the child in us and "grow up" into serious, competitive, controlled, ambitious, and task-oriented adults.

Serious adults don't allow themselves to daydream or do something just for the sake of doing it. No wonder we get depressed—we have forgotten how to play. We have lost our childlike instinct for doing what comes naturally, responding to curiosity, absorbing the wonder of life, and delighting in just being.

We need to become like little children. Little children are unencumbered by the demands for success and accomplishment. Little children dare to be spontaneous, don't care what others think of them, and are still in touch with their fun-loving selves.

How easy it is for us to play with children. We allow ourselves to enter into their world and play, as long as everybody understands we are doing it for the sake of the children. In reality, being with children gives us an excuse to be playful. We like to sit and watch children play with each other because it is a beautiful sight to behold, but also because we play vicariously through children.

We will never be children again, but we can be childlike in our approach to life. We can allow ourselves to let go and frolic in the sun. We can stop ourselves from stifling the spontaneous moments of fun that come our way. We can allow ourselves times of silliness and frivolity.

Adult play may include a vacation or a visit with friends that involves plenty of fun and laughter. Play may include hobbies, sports, games, and other enjoyable activities. Mostly, however, playfulness is an attitude that we adopt toward life. It is a receptivity to the unexpected and unplanned, an openness to spontaneity. There is playfulness in each one of us that keeps us alive and well, if only we let it be expressed.

Pruning

We want to enjoy the fruit of spring without suffering through the barren winter. We want to receive the new without having to give up the old. But we will not receive a return without first making an investment. We will not experience growth until we have first been pruned.

This death-and-resurrection cycle is not limited to the physical realm of life, but holds true in the social, psychological, and spiritual realms as well.

Families are in constant transition. Spouses must be acutely aware of the dynamic state of their relationship if it is to survive. Both must be willing to let go of the old, unmet expectations that have now turned into demands. Both must understand that the other is changing with every passing day and that this is a natural progression they need not fear or stifle.

Spouses must be willing to release themselves and each other from old roles and find new ways to reach for their full human potential.

As children grow, the relationship they have with their parents must also grow. Parents must not continue to treat children as six-year-olds when they are teenagers, or as teenagers when they are young adults. Parents must gradually let go of their "babies" and recognize their children as men-and-women-in-the-making.

As we move into new phases of life, it is

not so much the new and different that frightens us as the letting go of the old and familiar. "Doesn't anything stay the same?" we ask desperately. To be pruned is painful.

When we refuse to release our hold on the old, we get stuck between the past and the present. It is only when we are willing to allow death to come to what was, and to grieve it adequately, that we can welcome the new buds of life.

Death and resurrection are the essence of our spirituality. Day by day, moment by moment, we die to ourselves so that God may live in and through us. It is not a matter of killing off parts of ourselves, but of releasing that which is not life-giving and embracing that which is. It is a courageous act of turning away from that which distracts us and turning to God with a singleness of heart, much as a flower looks to the sun for life.

The death that comes to our self-sufficiency, our self-importance, and our self-hatred gives birth to a life of co-creation, humility, and love.

Purpose

Common to all of us is the purpose that is inherent in our humanity: to love God with our whole being and to let God live through us. From this universal purpose comes an individual purpose for each of us. From this purpose we draw our values and meaning.

Our purpose in life colors all that we do, all that we experience, and all that we are. Even suffering can be given meaning and turned into an agent of growth. Philosopher

Friedrich Nietzsche believed that the person "who knows a 'why' for living will surmount every 'how.'"

Confronted with overwhelming demands, some of us lose sight of our purpose. Others of us have never known it. In either case, we flounder like a ship without a rudder, letting life happen to us and then reacting from a scattered self.

Sometimes a crisis or major loss forces us to begin to clarify what is important and what is not. Clarity can also come to us through serious introspection and prayer of the heart. However it is that we arrive at an answer, it is imperative that we ask ourselves: "What is my purpose in life? What motivates me? For what do I live? For what would I be willing to die?"

Happiness cannot be our purpose in life. Peace cannot be our purpose. Pleasure or power cannot fulfill us. Fulfillment is not something we can get through diligent or aggressive pursuit. We become fulfilled as a result of reaching beyond ourselves. Our purpose gives us a mark at which to aim, and even if we never hit it, we can be fulfilled in the effort because through it we will have stretched, changed, developed, and grown. Life is an ascent to the highest potential of our humanity. Either we embark on the climb or we wither and die at the foothills.

The paradox of life is that if we seek out our purpose, we will never find it. We cannot buy it, and it cannot be given to us by other people. Our purpose comes to us through our spiritual self; it is given to us by God. It is born of the nature of who we are. Our purpose has to do with our personality, our experiences in life, our circumstances, talents, interests, emotions, thoughts, and most of all, with our belief in God and God's will for us.

Many of us are stressed because we have taken on too much and are pulled in too many directions. But even more dangerous is a lack of tension in life because of a loss of purpose.

If life is meaningless, we will fall into depression and may even contemplate suicide. We need the healthy tension that comes to a life lived with intention. We need to be challenged by life, and as we respond with freedom and creativity, we are fulfilled.

Purpose gives us the enthusiasm to do what we must do. Purpose gives us the conviction to sacrifice when necessary. Purpose gives meaning to our suffering, to our living, and ultimately to our dying.

Whether life is a task that we are obligated to perform or a mission to which we are dedicated depends on us. When we decide to lose ourselves in a purpose beyond ourselves, then we find ourselves, and this gives ultimate meaning to life.

Quiet

Quiet is more than the absence of noise. It is a state of being that allows us to come to a complete stop, to settle, and to hear the voice of God.

To be quiet is to enter the harbor during the tempest, to be protected, restored, soothed, and healed before we embark again on the difficult journey of life. It is not an escape from the demands of life, but rather a way we can garner the forces to meet those demands. Quiet heals us in body, mind, and spirit.

To still the body is to let it come to rest, release it from the tension of activity, give it the time it needs to regenerate. The quiet body is like a babe in the arms of its Mother God, drinking in nourishment and just letting itself be.

We can quiet the body by sitting still in a place apart from the rest of the world. We can quiet the body by relaxing the muscles in our stomach and releasing the tension in our brow and jaw. We can quiet the body by breathing deeply and slowly until our external self is congruent with our internal self.

To still the mind is to give it repose from the struggle between polarities and to let it float in the oneness to which it belongs. The quiet mind is open and attentive to the whisper that is uttered from within. It is receptive to inspiration and available to creativity.

The quiet mind taps the reservoir of universal knowledge that is not accessible to the cluttered or busy mind. At the center of the quiet mind, things fall into place and sense is found. It is here that we can grasp what we need to know because first we have to let it go. The quiet mind surrenders its will and waits to learn the pleasure of God.

We can quiet the mind through listening prayer, through meditation, or by allowing it to just *be* as we do manual work or perform repetitive activity.

To still the spirit is to let ourselves be grounded in the reality of life. We quiet the spirit when we cease to fly in every direction looking for signs of God, and instead are willing to land among the ordinary and mundane, where we find, not signs of God, but God.

We quiet the spirit when we relinquish control over our illumination, when we leave it to God alone to save us from ourselves. We quiet the spirit when we trust in the unconditional love of God and God's sometimes mysterious ways of showing that love to us. We quiet the spirit when we realize that it is

not we who quiet us, but God responding to
our inherent need for the stillness of the soul.

Receiving

Some say that it is more blessed to give than to receive, yet the truth is that we have nothing to give until first we have received.

In our society we have been socialized by our families, schools, and churches to give of ourselves until it hurts. We have been made to believe that the virtuous thing to do is to spend ourselves completely on others, through either work or the family. We have been well trained in the art of giving, but in

the process we have forgotten the art of re-
ceiving.

We have concluded that if we continue to
give, we will be loved and accepted by those
who receive from us. When this doesn't happen, we do not reevaluate our conclusion; we
merely give more.

We all want to be loved and accepted by
others. These are basic human needs. But consider how loved and accepted babies are, and
all they do is receive. As they receive they
prompt in others the need to give, and they
obtain for themselves what they will give
away tomorrow.

It is as blessed to receive as to give. After
all, what could be more indicative of our true
nature as poor, empty, broken, and needy people? We are incomplete and will not be made
whole until we are willing to receive the love
God gives us directly and through each other.

Our blessedness comes not from the pride
of giving beyond our limitations, but from the

humility to receive the gifts of God and use them according to God's will. Our blessedness comes not from our sacrifice to God and others, but from our willingness to participate in the economy of love.

The law of this economy is that we cannot give away what we do not have. Unless we first receive comfort or mercy, we cannot comfort or forgive others. Unless we first receive our inheritance as children of God, we cannot share it with others.

Let us learn that it is more important to realize the extent of our neediness than to practice generosity and that it is more crucial to focus on the quality of what we receive than on what we offer.

Let us love God enough to receive God's unconditional love and forgiveness and God's beautiful world with all its creatures. Let us love ourselves enough to receive our own forgiveness, appreciation, sense of worthiness, and kindness. Let us love others enough to receive from them whatever they would give us.

Rejection

Whether real or imagined, rejection is a painful experience that we attempt to avoid at all costs. The problem is that sometimes the cost is our own rejection of ourselves.

Usually our fear of rejection stems from early childhood memories of having been rejected. Even when we don't remember the specific incident, we remember how horrible it felt. We decided early on to do anything we could to keep rejection from hurting us again.

It doesn't matter whether those who rejected us meant to or not. What matters is how it appeared to us and how we reacted to it at the time.

Take the case of a young child who is treated with all the love and attention he could want during his first year of life, only to be suddenly cast off because a new child has come onto the scene with a chronic physical ailment. The parents spend all of their time, energy, and attention on the ailing child. The neglected child does not understand that his parents must tend to the ailing child and does not take into account his parents' limitations. The child only knows that once he was embraced and cherished, and now he feels cast aside in favor of somebody else. The child does not reason that his parents are doing the best they can but only experiences the pain of rejection.

Consider another child whose parents are forced by economic circumstances to work outside the home. It does not matter to the child that her parents are working so that she can eat and have a roof over her head. She believes only that if Mommy and Daddy are always gone, it must be her fault. She must have done something wrong to make them go away.

There are many other examples of physical and emotional unavailability on the part of parents due to alcoholism, workaholism, divorce, and other dysfunctional family situations. Whatever the specific situation, the bottom line for a child is that he or she is left out in the cold.

Why does rejection hurt so much? It has to do with how we understand rejection. For most of us, to be rejected means that we are not loved, and nothing hurts more in life than to feel unloved. Rejection means that we are not worthy to be included in the life of another, that something is wrong with us, that we must be guilty of something, that we are different and don't really belong—that we are not wanted, period.

Our fear of rejection follows us throughout life and damages our relationships. We may decide to try to constantly please others so that they will not reject us. We will go out of our way to be what they want us to be and do what they want us to do. We will avoid all forms of conflict or confrontation lest they lead to rejection. In the process, of course, we reject ourselves and opt instead to become the persons we believe others want us to be. Having rejected ourselves, we live life outside ourselves.

We may decide to place thick walls around us to protect us from the pain of rejection. We are careful not to form intimate relationships, invest in others, or trust anyone. This way, others don't have the chance to reject us.

Sometimes we conclude that if we expect others to reject us, it won't hurt so much when it happens. The problem here is that we end up bringing rejection about in order to fit our script. Then we can say, "See, I told you I would be rejected."

However we play out our fear of rejection, there is a little child within each of us who yearns to be loved, accepted, and included. It is this part of us that provides us with the hope to change. It is to this part that we, as adults, must direct truckloads of love. We need to do for ourselves what we have wanted others to do for us. It is imperative that we parent ourselves in such a way that we begin to feel valued, wanted, respected, and chosen.

To love ourselves means that we first acknowledge our condition as a wounded person who still reacts out of a fear of rejection. Through self-love, we can come to understand ourselves better and gently coach ourselves to find healthier ways to react to rejection. Self-love will turn us inward, where we can be ourselves without fearing rejection. Self-love will heal us of our childhood wounds. As we begin to accept ourselves, we gain the courage to risk being both vulnerable and assertive with others. This risk will be the beginning of a new life.

Remembering

*E*ven as we step into new life, one foot is still planted in the past. As we change our life direction, we must still contend with what has been.

The temptation is to walk away from yesterday as though it never happened. We want to deny it and begin anew, but we cannot rebuild with permanence unless we determine the composition of our foundation.

The key to improving our way of life is not a curtain that falls between who we have been and who we will become. It is a bridge that connects one with the other. No matter how much we try to leave the past behind, we come to realize that we bring it with us. While we don't have to dwell on our history, we need to remember it in order to create a better future.

If we have been broken in days gone by, it is only by remembering what happened to us that we will begin to heal. Remembering means putting the pieces of ourselves back together as we work toward wholeness and a happier, healthier life.

Remembering can be painful. We would rather not revisit the past, even in our minds. Yet, our memories are the keys that unlock the mystery of our present selves. Understanding why we are as we are allows us to decide how we will respond to life now and in the future.

Some of us have neatly hidden away the past, lest it interfere with what is going on today. But although the past may be hidden from the conscious self, it has not been hidden from the unconscious self, and, in fact, continues to affect every aspect of life. To remember is to bring the hidden to light, where it can be acknowledged and dealt with constructively.

Growth means letting go of something old and taking hold of something new. But we cannot let go of what we are not conscious of. Only by bringing the past into the present can we effectively release it. Once it is released, we are free to move on.

In order to heal and grow from the past, we need to tell our stories. We remember by talking to ourselves and others about the events in our lives. Remembering pleasant as well as unpleasant times helps us to remove blind spots from our vision. We need to fill in the picture of the past as honestly as possible in order to live truthfully today.

When we see more clearly what happened to us, we are in a better position to forgive

ourselves. Understanding more completely
how we were shaped, we are able to let go of
the guilt that has plagued us and the shame
that has confined us to our lesser selves.

By remembering the past, no matter how
dark, and integrating it into the present, no
matter how painful, we become responsible
for our lives. We do not wallow in self-pity,
nor do we waste our time blaming others for
our lives. Instead, we accept what has been,
acknowledge what is, and determine for ourselves what will be.

Sacrifice

It is in giving up something precious for the sake of a higher good that we discover our capacity to love. Whether we sacrifice to protect the welfare of another or to promote a cause beyond ourselves, we are transformed by the act.

Carl Jung wrote, "It is only through the mystery of self-sacrifice that a man may find himself anew."

Sacrifice is a mystery because we do not truly understand its healing power. The paradox is that in giving, we receive; in surrendering, we conquer; in being pruned, we blossom; and in dying, we live. We find ourselves anew because our identity is made known to us according to that which we are willing to release and the purpose for which we are willing to release it.

Some of us bring burnt offerings to the altar of life in the form of self-abuse and unsolicited sacrificial acts designed not to manifest our love, but rather to gain control or elicit favor from God or others.

Some of us sacrifice constantly in the name of unselfishness and love, but we do it to boost our sagging egos or to obligate others to us. In our unhealthy sacrifice, we try to meet our needs by abusing ourselves, and we end up resenting those for whom we have supposedly sacrificed.

When in our sacrifice we give *up* ourselves instead of give *of* ourselves, chances are we are into unhealthy sacrifice. Healthy sacrifice is an expression of love and concern. It is a courageous act that is usually done at great loss to the one who sacrifices and great gain to the one for whom the sacrifice is made.

In healthy sacrifice, we do not feel used nor do we believe that others owe us for our sacrifice. When we sacrifice from love, we take full responsibility for our decision and expect no return, credit, or sympathy.

Sacrifice is not an end in itself; it is part of the process of healthy living. Sacrifice in and of itself is not a virtue; it is a consequence of loving much.

Sadness

*S*adness is a healthy
and useful emotion, yet we sometimes do not
appreciate it and even run away from it. Much
is written about ways to be happy and joyful
but little about the legitimacy of sadness and
the contribution it makes to life.

Sadness is looked upon as something to be
overcome or gotten rid of, but without sadness
we would not be able to experience an important part of our humanity. Without sadness
we would not know the valleys of our being.

Sadness is a feeling that overcomes us when we tap into the pain of our reality. It allows us to face the tragedies of life as they really are, or were, and to lament them fully.

Sadness is part of grief and grief is part of sadness, but they are not the same. In grief, our experience is one of loss. In sadness, we experience the pain of what is and of what will be. Sadness is also not the same as depression. In depression we come to an emotional halt, but sadness is a more active emotion, one that moves us from one point to another.

Sadness has many sources. We may be sad because of what we see before us: an old woman crippled by disease, a child abandoned or abused, a home divided by divorce, a lake polluted, a nation at war, a people scattered and confused, a world without peace.

We can feel sadness for others or for the state of world affairs. But perhaps the most profound sadness we can feel is the sadness for ourselves.

We may regret the way things have turned out. We would have wanted them to be different. Yet things went awry, the unexpected happened, and we were left where we didn't want to be. We are saddened as we acknowledge what we have missed in life and recognize the holes that are left unfilled.

We are saddened when we anticipate trouble, suffering, or death in the coming days. Imminent separation from those we love also brings us profound sorrow.

The sadness we feel for ourselves is not to be confused with feeling sorry for ourselves. Self-pity has its place, but it must be limited in scope and time lest we become stuck in a pattern of "woe is me." Sadness goes beyond self-pity. Unlike self-pity, which places us in a victim role, sadness is a cleanser of the soul. It allows us to experience and express our deepest emotions and integrate them into the whole self.

In sadness we no longer need to remain a

victim. Having acknowledged and lamented the circumstances that hurt us and having become aware of that impact on our lives, we can now move forward, still wounded, but in the process of healing.

It is not enough to feel our sadness. The way to wholeness is to share that which is within. We must be willing to talk about our sadness with someone who cares. And as we tell another why we are sad, we feel the sadness more completely, and it is able to do its work in us.

Let us not hide from sadness or its sources. Let us not run from the pain that must come as we face the reality of life. Let us be willing to stay in our sadness for as long as it takes to work through it.

Security

S ecurity is an illusion, yet our quest for it is perennial. For some of us, security is a god that we worship with all of our thoughts, emotions, and actions. It seems we would do anything in order to be secure. Our inordinate preoccupation with security immobilizes us and keeps us from risking and living freely.

We are ready to trade the kingdom of heaven for something on which we believe we can count or some assurance of protection in life. But there is no such thing as security and nothing is guaranteed us, not even things we ask from God. This is a hard lesson for us to learn, and we keep on reaching for that sense of security that is never there.

We say to ourselves: if only we can save enough money, we will be secure; if only we take care of ourselves, we will be healthy; if only we work hard enough, we will keep our jobs; if only we protect our families, they will be safe from harm; and if only we pray enough, God will take care of us. All of these "if only's" depend upon *our* action, *our* will, *our* intellect, *our* power, and *our* faith; consequently, none of them can guarantee the acquisition or retention of security. None of them takes into account the powers that are beyond our control.

Bars on windows may keep us secure against intruders, but they cannot protect us from the hurricane that comes out of nowhere and levels the house. Investing many hours and much energy in our jobs may prevent us from getting fired for incompetence, but it cannot protect us from getting laid off due to an unexpected economic crunch. We can take precautions to protect our health by eating right, but we cannot fend off the insidious threat of a killer cancer. And try as we may to be safe in all we do, we remain vulnerable to accidents caused by others.

No matter how much we rely on our will, intellect, or power, we will not know security. Yet, some of us depend so much on the security we think the world can give us that we are devastated when it doesn't come. We know only too well the sense of insecurity that overwhelms us following a major catastrophe. We are left hurt, lost, and distrustful. We learn quickly that no one is immune from life's tragic turns. We discover that, in the final analysis, there is nothing concrete to hold on to through the storm. Here we begin to let go of the illusion of security and to entrust our fate to the will of God. Only on God do we come to depend.

Our faith consists no longer in believing that we can protect ourselves or that God will protect us from all harm, but in believing that God will stay with us through all that comes and will provide us with what we need to overcome harm. Our faith becomes focused, not on security, but on the knowledge that God will not abandon us. We learn that we cannot take anything in life for granted except the unconditional love of God and that God's love is all we really need. That is our treasure; that is our security.

Shame

We were born without shame, completely happy with ourselves. It is when someone told us that we were naked—that is, that we fell short of expectations—that we encountered shame for the first time.

We acquired shame in the early years of life. Shame-based messages from parents, teachers, and other adults left us feeling worthless, defective, inadequate, and humiliated. At times, even our feelings were discounted. We may have been allowed to feel hurt, but it was not all right to feel anger, loneliness, or depression. Shame may also have come from our being abused physically, sexually, and/or emotionally, or from neglect. The shame may have been directed at only one part of us, but it eventually affected our entire identity. Soon we were hiding a seemingly defective identity from ourselves and others. We dared not look into anyone's eyes lest he or she discover how bad we really were.

We were not respected as human beings if our boundaries were violated when we were children or adolescents. Sometimes when the violation was so unbearable, we suppressed full memory of it as well as accompanying emotions. What was not suppressed was the shame from being violated in such a way. We may also have come to believe that we were responsible in some way for the violation.

If we were neglected by or separated from

those we loved because we were "bad," our shame is also related to the fear of abandonment. We carry this shame-based separation anxiety with us into adulthood.

Shame-based adults are especially sensitive to criticism and react to it with a vengeance. Our shame keeps us separated from others, from ourselves, and from God. We are afraid of being exposed, so we hide behind overachievement, inordinate introversion, addictive behaviors, and other masks. As shame-based persons, we develop a need to control the environment so that we will not be humiliated again.

Shame-based persons resist commitment because it may mean that we will be found out by those to whom we commit. "If they only knew..." we say to ourselves in fear. Intimacy is out of the question because with intimacy comes the sharing of our reality with others, and we dare not risk that.

The additional tragedy is that we pass our

shame-based behavior on to our children.

To rid ourselves of the shame that has plagued us since youth, we need to get in touch with our emotions. It's all right, for instance, to get angry at those who have shamed us, whether or not they meant to do so. Our anger and resentment, if experienced and expressed appropriately, can empower us to take back our lives. One way to do this is to write a strongly worded letter to the person involved and then tear it up. Another way is to do anger therapy with a professional. Somehow the suppressed emotions must be dealt with.

We also need to ask ourselves, "Whose shame is it, anyway?" After we identify the persons who shamed us, we can decide to return the shame to them.

We can begin to let go of our shame by risking exposure of who we really are—warts and all—with someone we trust. We need to let go of our shame through self-forgiveness and eventually through forgiveness of those who shamed us. We also need to replace, little by little, all those negative and shame-filled messages with supportive and encouraging messages to ourselves. Positive affirmations are helpful here.

We also must begin to rebuild the boundaries that were violated by others. These are not the same as the walls that we have built up as a result of our shame. They are the boundaries we all need in order to maintain an individual identity.

Above all, we need to remember that God created us without shame and loves us unconditionally. We need to continuously tap this source of hope, encouragement, and pride in who we are.

Shoulds

We all fall short of the *should*s we impose on ourselves, yet we mercilessly continue to say that we *should* be able to do this or that and that we *should* not feel or think the way we do.

We adopt standards that others have imposed on us or that we have taken upon ourselves, and we berate ourselves regularly for not living up to them. Our expectations sometimes border on fantasy. We criticize ourselves, saying we *should* be more loving, more composed, more ambitious, more or less emotional, more giving. We say to ourselves that we *should* accomplish more, not get angry, get over our grief more quickly, have more faith, read more, eat less, exercise more, watch television less, and on and on.

The list of *should*s is inexhaustible, and we draw on it to remind ourselves how bad we really are. We are always ready to join the chorus of past voices in our head that tell us we're not doing or being enough. How insensitive and unkind we are to ourselves when we fail to recognize that most of the time we do the best we can with what we have.

Sometimes the best we can do is make it out of bed in the morning. At other times we are able to make grand contributions to the world. The efforts are equal in the eyes of God if in both cases we are giving all we've got.

We are compelled by love of self to accept ourselves wherever we happen to be and to appreciate whatever we are able to muster. To judge ourselves harshly because we cannot deliver more than we have comes of pride. To accept our limitations—and the gifts we offer in spite of those limitations—is humility.

Silence

*T*he time has come for us to retreat from noise and activity. We have given much, and now we must be willing to receive.

The call to silence is not one we answer easily. We are so accustomed to noise that we feel out of control or insecure when we are not making it or being absorbed by it.

Imagine being quiet, even for a moment. What a helpless feeling for those of us who use words to control and manipulate the world around us. What vulnerability for those of us who prefer to hide behind chatter and clatter, lest we be left alone with God.

We are so busy transmitting that we dare not stop long enough to receive. We don't trust enough to be silent. Yet, it is in silence that we hear the voice of God.

We are afraid to enter into silence because it is a descent into poverty as well. When we dare to be quiet, we discover how little we really possess. We come to realize that what has been demanding our attention has left us with nothing. It has distracted us from everything that matters.

Silence threatens our very existence because we have for too long identified *being* with noise and activity. By allowing silence to envelop us in the midst of the noise, we surrender to the activity of God, become receptive to what God would give to us, and touch a reality that goes beyond the senses.

The noise that has our attention is not limited to what we hear through our ears. We are also plagued by wounded memories, anxious thoughts, and the loneliness that comes from the belief that life is meaningless.

Even our futile and presumptuous attempts to understand God are noises of the mind that drown out the silence of the heart. To go beyond our habitual consciousness, we must move toward the center of the heart and embrace the God who dwells therein.

It may seem like emptiness in the beginning, but in the desert of the heart we are given a deeper awareness of hidden things. We no longer seek revelation in the silence of the mind. We are merely receptive and revelation comes.

We must be careful not to neglect our bodies as we become silent. There must be a letting go of the physical being that allows integration and centeredness. We need to be physically relaxed, and we need a quiet place to wait for God. We need to stay in the present

moment to enter a tranquil state of loving surrender.

Our spirituality and prayer become not a
speaking but a listening. We move from communication with God to communion with
God. We are held there in moments of deep
absorption. The prayer of the heart is silent because the language of love is silence.

Stress

*T*he stress in our lives is not the problem; how we choose to react to it is.

There is stress that we bring upon ourselves, such as that which results from unhealthy behavior, and we can avoid this stress by changing our behavior. But there is other stress that we cannot avoid and over which we have little or no control. It is for this inevitable stress that we must develop an effective coping strategy.

S — Self-Love
T — Time
R — Rest, Recreation, Restoration
E — Exercise
S — Settling
S — Spirituality

Self-love comes from God's unconditional
love for us. First and foremost, we must look
to God for love. Let us ask for the grace to love
God with our whole being, for the openness to
receive God's love for us, and for the ability to
love ourselves.

We can handle the stress of life when we
are loving ourselves enough to take care of
ourselves. This means that we treat ourselves
kindly, considerately, and gently. It means
that we encourage ourselves through af-
firming self-talk and that we forgive ourselves
for our mistakes. Self-love motivates us to protect ourselves from harm, accept ourselves as
we are, and be fair to ourselves. Through self-

love we see ourselves in all humility and set our goals and expectations in accordance with that reality. We let go of those issues over which we don't have control and focus on those over which we do. Self-love gives us the energy we need to cope with stress.

Time can work for or against us, depending on what we choose to do with it. We can allow ourselves to procrastinate and then rush to meet deadlines, we can leave little time to finish big projects, and we can hurry from one activity to another without taking a moment to catch a breath or utter a prayer. But when we manage our time by setting priorities and planning accordingly, we stay directed and live a purposeful life. We need to consider time in the light of eternity. It is a precious commodity and must be used wisely, yet we must not be so jealous of it that we become constricted in our living. Let us take the time that abundant living requires.

Rest, recreation, and **restoration** are God's

way of giving us new life. When we stop to rest, we allow our physical, mental, and emotional selves to regain lost energy. Rest, including adequate sleep, is vital to our creativity and to our readiness to serve God.

Recreation brings to life the child within that is free, spontaneous, and joyful. By allowing ourselves to play, we are being re-created, made over, renewed. Fun and laughter are great antidotes to the stress that sometimes overwhelms us. Finding ways to relax, whether in play, manual work, or creativity, takes us out of our seriousness and lets the soul rest.

Exercise must be mentioned as part of a stress coping strategy because not all of us have enough physical movement in our lives to stay healthy. We are physical beings and need to use what we have been given. Our exercise should stretch us a little, include a wide range of motion, be regular, and be aerobic in nature. The rigor and stress the body experiences during exercise ward off the kind of stress that can be a silent killer. Coping with stress by caring for the physical self also necessitates responsible use of all drugs, including caffeine, nicotine, and alcohol.

Settling is a way to cope with stress. To settle for too little is itself very stressful, but to be willing to settle for, say, eighty percent of what we want in a given situation is being realistic and guards against perfectionistic tendencies. Settling means that we see what is, rather than the ideal we would have it be, and that we work with what exists to the best of our ability. To face reality and live within it means that we set goals that are realistic and achievable. We may need to let go of some unfulfilled dreams, make adjustments, and renegotiate life. From settling comes a deep appreciation for what we have and an ability to build on it.

Spirituality is the most important element of all and permeates everything else. Spirituality means acknowledging the transcendent self, that part of us that is not limited to the physical, intellectual, and emotional. Spirituality is our sense of belonging to God completely and of God's life in us. We converse with God through prayer, and it is through prayer that God soothes, heals, and guides us. Our main purpose in life is to love and be loved by God. When we remember this, all else is relegated to a lesser place, and our stress is manageable.

Suffering

*T*o enter into the garden of suffering is to enter into the mystery of transformation.

It is all right that we are at first overwhelmed by our suffering and become angry, desperate, and tired. It is all right that we are tempted to despair. What matters is that we wait long enough in prayer to receive grace. When we have reached our limits and exhausted our strength and courage, we are reinforced from deep within. Then we tap the power of the God who is in us, and we come to know that whatever happens, we are not alone.

Our heart feels empty and pain reaches into our core. From this hell we consecrate our life to God. Our response to the God of unconditional love reveals to us the secret of life: no matter how much we suffer, God is in us and with us and will never leave us. With this foundation under us, we can fall only so far; with this belief in our heart, all else pales in significance.

In life we suffer tribulations, but we must not despair, for we are not abandoned in our plight. Always there is the God who loves us unconditionally; always there is the God who gives us comfort and encouragement.

God's comfort and encouragement allow us to accept our suffering and its impact on us. We no longer fight it; we do not refuse it; we let it come upon us to do its work. As we live through our suffering, it loses its power over us and becomes a part of who we are. To accept our suffering is not to be resigned to it but to actively absorb it and let it work for the glory of God. In this way the agony and the glory become one.

The comfort we receive from God comes in the form of a new perspective. We gain strength and courage by releasing from our grasp that which can die and cling to that which never will. We gain strength and courage from our belief in a love so potent that sorrow, pain, and even death cannot overcome it.

Our fear of suffering and our resistance to it produce more suffering than is necessary. Only when we enter into our vulnerability and allow to come what is to come will our suffering transform us. The worst hell is the one we create when, in our attempt to avoid suffering, we refuse to live and love.

The suffering that we endure is not a punishment from God. Rather, when we suffer the atrocities that sometimes come with life and remain steadfast in our love and dependence on God, we are blessed in our suffering. Through it we discover a faith we did not know we had, we draw closer to God, and we are transformed in such a way that we are in this world but no longer of it.

Suffering is not something we need to pursue. It is not a virtue. By itself it has no value. It is a consequence of love, part of the nature of life.

How we choose to respond to suffering is what matters. For, as with all the circumstances of life, we have the freedom to decide how to respond. We have the freedom to transcend suffering by finding meaning in it. And we find meaning by accepting suffering for the sake of another, ourselves, God, or a cause in which we believe. In our pain, our hopelessness, our darkest hour, we may fulfill the meaning of life.

Suffering, even unto death, calls us out of a stagnant self and shakes us from our attachments to the temporal. As nothing else can, suffering compels us to transcend the state of being half-alive and move toward abundant life.

In suffering we come to know the extent of our poverty and powerlessness. Then the fervor of our love for God can overcome even the greatest of life's pains. Always God is present in our being; always God calls us to a higher plane.

Time Alone

*S*ometimes we work such long hours in the service of others that we do not even take time for a proper meal. But the nourishment we crave goes beyond our need for food and rest. As we get in touch with the emptiness within and experience our dryness, we come to realize that it is the soul that hungers and thirsts.

Though we live our lives for God, we are not immune to physical, mental, and emotional exhaustion. We must eventually confront our limitations and discard the illusion that we are self-sufficient.

Getting away—letting go of the world and all it asks of us—brings rest to the soul. The tired body relaxes more profoundly than even in sleep. The mind dismisses the myriad distractions that keep it confused, and the emotions become more clear and alive. This integration of the spirit allows for the abundant life that is our inheritance.

But the demands of life do not respect the need for getting away. In fact, demands on us grow in proportion to our willingness to meet them, regardless of our ability to do so.

The time we need to be alone and to be nourished in the arms of God will not likely be found in the ordinary course of the day. It must be sought like a long-lost treasure. Once we recover it, we must guard it jealously from those who would steal it from us and leave us to die of spiritual starvation.

Sometimes it is those who love us most

who do not understand our need to be alone.
Yet, it is for them as much as for ourselves that
we must leave the crowd and not return until
our soul has been restored.

Our time away may not always be extensive. Sometimes we may be able to carve
only minutes of repose out of our entire day.
This will be sufficient if during our brief escape we focus on the spirit within. It is this focus that brings about our integration, if only
for a while.

Small segments of time will be enough for
our spiritual health if they are frequent and
consistent. Our time-outs must become a regular part of life.

When we remember that we can move
only because we have stopped, we can work
only because we have rested, we can give only
because we have received, and we can love
only because we have been loved, then we will
go again into the hills to be alone and pray.

Touch

*F*rom our earliest days, it is the sensation of being held and physically tended to that enables us to thrive against the greatest of odds. We are born with this most basic need—to be touched—and it stays with us throughout life.

For many of us the need to be touched in a loving manner has not been adequately met, either in infancy or in adulthood. Some of us have grown used to the lack of touch over the years and have concluded that we can get along without it. Others of us whose need for touch has gone unmet have become inordinately needy and attempt to get our need met in unhealthy ways.

Our true self yearns for the life-giving touch of another. We do not feel complete until we have made that physical contact with someone who genuinely cares for us. Touch is the nonverbal communication that tells us we are loved.

Through touch we are nourished and comforted. To be held in the arms of someone who loves us, to feel the safe protection and tenderness of someone who cares, is the greatest ecstasy of all. To hold and be held tightly and without reservation is to unleash the passion of God. Through our embrace flows the energy of God's unconditional love.

The language of touch tells us we are lovable, touchable, acceptable and accepted, wanted—that we are not alone. A gentle hug from a friend can break through the isolation and loneliness we are feeling. A compassionate hand on the shoulder helps us feel acknowledged and understood when we are hurting.

The gift of touch may come from a hand that reached out to another hand to make the vital connection between human beings. It may come from a hand that massages and rubs a weary back, a hand that strokes and soothes in therapeutic form. The gift of touch may involve a sweet caress or may come as a full embrace. Whatever the manner, whatever the occasion, the gift of touch brings healing and renewal.

Even as we see touch as a gift, we must be careful to respect the physical boundaries of others and to receive permission from those whom we would touch. Some people prefer to keep their distance, afraid to be touched. Some men are afraid to touch or be touched by other men. Some women are afraid that a physical gesture may have sexual motivations. This is especially true for those who are survivors of sexual abuse. It is important to be sensitive to the barriers that block the gift of touch, whatever they may be. Sometimes the most loving gesture is to refrain from touch.

Through touch we act on an inherent longing to be united with one another, to be bonded together in body as we are in spirit.

Trade-Offs

*L*ife is a series of trade-offs. We must learn to let go of some things in order to have others, to be willing to relinquish in order to keep.

We began to learn this lesson early in life. As we attempted our first steps, we learned that unless we let go of one grip, we could not reach for another. It was as difficult then as it is now to acknowledge that we cannot have it all. Many of us continue to refuse to admit our limitations.

237

Take the case of a woman who has a full-time job with much responsibility, which she performs well. She also has three children to raise, a home to run, and volunteer commitments to meet. She expects herself to come through in all areas of her life at one-hundred percent or more. Besides her need to succeed professionally, she feels her children must be a sign of her great parenting skills, her home must be picture-perfect all the time, and she must be full of loving energy as she carries out her duties. At no point does she ask whether she is capable of keeping all these tops spinning at the same time. And she wonders why she is always feeling exhausted.

Consider the case of a man who takes on one project after another at work without examining the consequences. He figures he'll get things done somehow, but soon he feels overwhelmed and overworked. He blames the day for not having enough hours to meet his needs. He doesn't recognize that the time

available is not the problem, but rather his unrealistic demands on himself that cause him to
burn out.

Trading-off is not something we do well. It
is difficult for us to admit that our time, energy, and attention are limited and that we
must live life accordingly. For every new en-
deavor we consider, we need to ask not "How
can I make this fit into my already crowded
schedule?" but rather "What am I willing to
give up?"

Sometimes we take on more tasks in the
name of God, and sometimes we do so because we enjoy being busy. Sometimes we
overburden ourselves because we believe others expect it of us. Regardless of our motivation for stretching ourselves thin, it works
against us and those we are attempting to
help. Eventually, something has to give.

When we allow ourselves to be humble,
that is, to be realistic about our resources, we
are apt to take on only what we can handle. As

the adage says, "Don't bite off more than you can chew" (to say nothing of swallowing!). When we take on more than we can adequately do, we suffer from a sense of grandiosity. Our humility tells us directly and plainly to get real. Our humility admonishes us to choose between options rather than try to perform beyond our means.

Just as we must choose between items we want at the store because our funds are limited, so we must choose between what we can and cannot realistically do because our time and energy are limited too. Sometimes we have no choice but to carry out several roles, as in the case of a parent who also works outside the home. In such cases, a trade-off must be made. The job is perhaps crucial for survival, and the children are of utmost importance, so let the house come third. Lower your expectations of how it must be kept up.

With humility we are able to choose one project to which we will devote our best effort and, at the same time, release our hold on other things we also want to do. To hang on to everything may mean that nothing will get done very well, if at all.

As we make our choices, we must grieve that which we have relinquished. The pruning we are willing to undergo will result in a harvest that is less in quantity but offers so much more in quality.

Unfinished Business

*O*ur external conflicts are reflected internally. When we are at odds with someone, chances are that we are at odds with a part of our inner self. And as we take care of unfinished business with our brothers and sisters, we can also achieve inner reconciliation.

Sometimes we can directly approach those with whom we need to reconcile. At other times, a direct approach may be counterproductive or out of the question.

When we no longer have access to the one who has hurt us or whom we have hurt, we can still deal with that person in our active imagination. We can write a letter of amends, forgiveness, and reconciliation and then destroy the letter. The result will be the same as if we had dealt directly with the person, as long as we are sincere about what we write.

Tending to unfinished business is difficult. It can be painful to remember the harm perpetrated on us. Sometimes that harm was done in early childhood, and these are difficult memories to resurrect.

Sexual abuse, physical abuse, emotional abuse, abandonment, and neglect are the kinds of wounds that some of us carry into adulthood. These are the secrets of the soul that keep us nonintegrated, that show up as unexplained depression and untraceable physical ailments.

To be reconciled with those who have hurt us involves more than just forgiving. It means that we must first hold them accountable for what they did or failed to do. It means that we must get in touch with the emotions that we felt when they hurt us, emotions that we probably suppressed. This may entail reliving the experience, and that can be excruciating. It means that once we have felt the emotions, we identify them and express them in some manner. It means that we must confront the perpetrators—in real life or in our imagination, whichever is more appropriate—and tell them of our hurt and resentment. It means that having dealt with the emotions, we may forgive. Sometimes it is best to seek professional help when entering into this process.

When we tend to our unfinished business, we become reconciled with the ghosts from our past, and we are at one with the world and with ourselves. Through reconciliation we are made whole.

Victimization

We have all been victimized in one way or another. Some of us have remained stuck in the victim role. Others of us have begun to break the chains of victimization.

We are victimized when we are adversely affected by someone's actions or situations over which we have no control. Some of us have been victims of extremely damaging physical, sexual, or emotional abuse, or all three. Some of us have been victims of neglect or abandonment or of a crippling disease or an accident. Some of us have been victimized by the dire circumstances of our lives. Whatever the source of our victimization, it has left us feeling broken, used, duped, violated, betrayed, and helpless.

Repeated victimization conditions us to believe that we have no power over what happens to us. We come to believe that all we can do is accept what comes. We surrender ourselves to the whims of those who would have their way with us.

With a victim mentality, we believe that we deserve the mistreatment we receive and that we are not worthy of being protected against victimization. As victims we say: "What's the point of complaining about something that's already happened? You can't change the past."

We try neither to escape nor to fight back; instead we wait for what we believe is inevitable. Our attitude becomes fatalistic and passive, leaving us wide open for more victimization.

Since victimization is so familiar to us, we let our expectations of it play out. We may seek relationships with those who are emotionally unavailable, have addictive personalities, or are dysfunctional in some way. In extreme cases, we hook up with those who batter and are emotional abusers. At work, we may allow ourselves to be overworked and underpaid or to be treated with disrespect. Most likely, our relationships will be with those who do not consider our needs to be very important. Victims, after all, need victimizers to complete the dynamic.

A general characteristic of persons stuck in the victim role is that we become our own worst oppressors. Since we believe we are not worthy of much, we give little to ourselves in the way of respect, thoughtfulness, or consideration. We may allow ourselves the luxury of a little whining, but we don't expect much to come of it. We do not love ourselves, and in some cases we hate ourselves—our bodies, our personalities, our existence, everything about us.

It's not that we choose to be stuck in a victim role. Rather, there is the compulsion to continue what we know. We are so well acquainted with the victim script that we are afraid to try anything new. We are trapped by the only way of life we know. Concepts like power, boundaries, trust, and security are foreign to us. Instead, we live within the confines of powerlessness, enmeshment, fear, and insecurity.

In the past we have been victimized against our will, but whether we continue to be victimized depends on us. It is not easy to break the vicious cycle of victimization, but it is possible if we are willing to ask for help.

This is perhaps the most difficult barrier to overcome. As victims we have believed that we are not deserving of help, but we cannot afford to wait until our beliefs change. We need to ask for help and be willing to receive it. Once we decide that we don't want to live as victims any longer, there are some steps we must be willing to take.

First and foremost, we must acknowledge that we act like victims and understand how this affects our daily living. We must admit that by ourselves we cannot overcome our victim mentality. We must look to the power of God within us for help.

Second, we must trace our victimization as far into the past as we can to discover its source. We must revisit, in our minds, the times we have been victimized and remember how we were affected. This means that we must feel the emotions that resulted, including sadness, grief, anger, and rage toward our victimizers. This re-experiencing of emotions, or, in some cases, this experiencing of them for the first time, can be excruciating. Many of us prefer to remain victims of the past rather than confront the past emotionally. We may have been situational victims once, but our failure to confront past victimization will keep us psychological victims indefinitely.

Third, we must take another look at the victimization that was imposed on us and assign meaning to it for ourselves. That is, we must look for what we can learn and how we can grow from it. Let our suffering not have been in vain.

And last, we must confront the victimizer within us who has taken the place of all previous victimizers we have known. Rather than working directly to eliminate the victimizer within, our task is to support, affirm, and otherwise encourage ourselves in such a way that the victimizer in us is neutralized.

Eventually, through self-love, we begin to treat ourselves as we should have been treated by others. In the past we were helpless; now, as adults, we can protect ourselves. In the past we considered ourselves unworthy of being advocated for; now we assert ourselves on our own behalf. In the past we blamed ourselves for what was done to us; now we place the blame with the victimizers and acknowledge that our victimization was beyond our control. In the past we saw our lot as having to passively endure our victimization; now we are prepared to take the responsibility for the quality of our life. In the past we felt stuck; now we can choose to alter our situation or to leave it altogether.

In the past we felt alone in our victimization; now we realize that we are not alone. Now we draw strength from God, from ourselves, and from those around us who are willing and able to help.

Work

We have an inherent
need to be productive and creative, and when
we are not, we wither. Our human nature is to
give of ourselves to the world, to contribute to
it by using the power of creativity that we
share with God. In this impulse to create, we
go out of ourselves and become lost in our en-
deavors.

But even the most peaceful souls among us
succumb to an insidious form of violence
when we deliver ourselves up to excessive ac-

tivity, to overwork, to the pulls and pushes of the world's expectations, to the worries and demands of life, and to the ambition of accomplishment.

A common affliction among men and women alike is the syndrome of compulsive overwork. Many of us have grown up believing that it is bad to be doing nothing, so we make sure we are always busy at our job and at home. We push ourselves *to do* because we are afraid *not to do.* We believe that we are justified by what we accomplish, instead of by what is accomplished in us.

This anxiety is based on the misconception that *doing* is *being.* The truth is that only by first *being* can we effectively *do.* But our intense activity acts as a protection against our existential insecurity. Although the horror of doing nothing has resulted in our getting much done, it has also deprived us of one of God's gifts—the gift of just being.

We must learn that no matter what we do

in this achievement-oriented world, we are
building on sand. If we are to prevent disillusionment, our actions must be the consequences of who we are, not the other way
around.

Prayer suffers in a continuously busy life.
To listen to God we need to stop listening to
the order of the day. To receive from God we
need to empty our hands of tools. Staying
busy all the time keeps us from being available to our loved ones as well.

Our attitude toward doing nothing is als
responsible for the difficulty we have in tak
the time we need to rest. We usually wait ı
we collapse from exhaustion or illness bef
we allow ourselves resting time.

It is hard to break the habit of stayinɡ
busy. There is so much to do. Staying bı
believe, means survival, making money
ing on top of things, defending ourselⱱ
against a world that will pounce on us
are idle.

257

But even in our work we can find rest. We can work and not be tired if we work in cooperation with God. Work can be the vehicle of peace if it doesn't overwhelm us. Most jobs are complex and involved. To try to climb the entire mountain in one single bound is to bring defeat right from the start. One step at a time, one ledge at a time, one phase at a time is the secret to getting any job done. What is large is made small through the humility of our approach; the complex is made simple through the patience of our effort.

We must work in such a way that we are able to give our full attention to one job at a time. To work in disorder and disarray is to invite chaos and distraction. Lack of order makes us work harder and less effectively. It tires us out mentally and discourages us emotionally, and emotional resistance is a major cause of fatigue. Rather than turn away from a job that we must do, let us face it with enthusiasm and prayerfulness.

The nature of our work is not as important as our willingness to perform it with full intent and dedication. Regardless of how large or small the circle of our influence, what matters is our decision to do the best we can at what we do. We no longer work under the illusion that we must be best or first at something in order to matter to ourselves or others. In peace we accept ourselves as we are and appreciate our effort for what it is, and leave the rest to God.